# THERE'S MORE TO FISHING

## (Than Catching Fish)

**Tom Alkire**

# THERE'S MORE TO FISHING

## (Than Catching Fish)

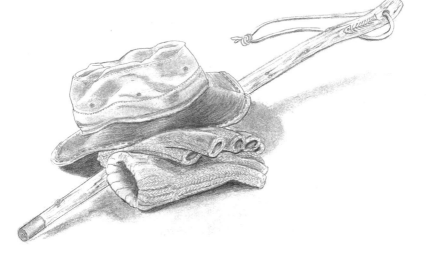

**Tom Alkire**

*Illustrations by Dürten Kampmann*

This book is dedicated to Dyann
for understanding....

# ACKNOWLEDGMENTS

Without the friendship and care of a large number of people, both on the water and off, this book would not have been possible. Frank Amato, the book's publisher, stands at the head of the list with his enthusiasm for this project from its beginning. Various other editors over the years have been encouraging including Ron Buel, Richard Meeker, Mark Zusman and Barry Johnson at *Willamette Week,* Chuck Wechsler at *Sporting Classics,* James Babb at *Gray's Sporting Journal* and Marty Sherman at *Flyfishing.*

Other acknowledgments go to my father who first showed me the path and didn't realize how full bore I'd go charging down it. More thanks to my mother, brothers, wife, children, Bill Bakke, Roscoe and Ray Funkhouser, Paul Pintarich, Dave Hughes, Tad Sweet, Mike O'Bryant, Bill Compton, Christy Wykoff, Michael Carey, Cal Cole, Rick Hafele, Barry Grimes, Mark Skolnick, Fred Scott, Leo Bustad, Izaak Walton, Drew Douglas, Brian Lockett and many members of The Anglers' Club of Portland.

**Published in 2000 by Frank Amato Publications, Inc.**
P.O. Box 82112, Portland, Oregon 97282
(503) 653-8108 • www.amatobooks.com

Hardbound ISBN: 1-57188-206-5
Hardbound UPC: 0-66066-00420-8

Illustrations: Dürten Kampmann

Printed in Singapore

10  9  8  7  6  5  4  3  2  1

# Contents

*Introduction* ........................................................ 11

*I.* THE SOCIABLE ANGLER ................................... 17

*II.* THE WELL-TRAVELED ANGLER ....................... 39

*III.* THE HOMEWATER ANGLER ............................ 57

*IV.* THE WELL-DRESSED ANGLER ......................... 75

*V.* THE WELL-FED ANGLER ................................... 87

*VI.* THE SPIRITED ANGLER .................................... 99

*VII.* THE NATURALIST ANGLER ............................ 109

*VIII.* THE UNTRUTHFUL ANGLER ......................... 129

*IX.* THE ROMANTIC ANGLER ................................ 143

*X.* THE AGING ANGLER ........................................ 157

*XI.* THE FIRESIDE ANGLER .................................. 169

# INTRODUCTION

As THE WELL-READ ANGLER KNOWS, THE BEDROCK OF THE angling soul was created more than three hundred years ago when Izaak Walton wrote *The Compleat Angler*. There are few books, on any topic, that have seen as many editions as *The Compleat Angler,* first published in 1653 and in print continuously since 1750. Copies of the book can be found in the libraries of English estates and alongside Montana trout streams. Some who have read the book fished with horsehair lines and greenheart rods, others fished with graphite rods and monofilament leaders unknown and unimagined in Walton's time.

And as most any serious fly fisherman will tell you, Walton was not much of a fly angler. Much of what he wrote about flies was borrowed from others such as from Leonard Mascall's *Booke of Fishing with Hooke and Line* published in 1600. The last edition of *The Compleat Angler* published in Walton's lifetime in 1676 included a section on fly fishing by Walton's younger friend, Charles Cotton, and while instructive on the art of taking fish with fur and feathers it lacks, at least for me, Walton's infective zest for life, his mirthful style.

While Walton writes about all manner of fishes and how to catch them, his book's enduring popularity is not because of his excellent instructions on how to make a paste of rabbit flesh, bean-flour and honey for catching carp. He is remembered for his colorful rendering of angling as the contemplative man's pursuit, for showing us how to live more than how to fish.

Today, many would consider Walton a lazy, windbag of an angler. There he is sitting under a streamside sycamore tree, quoting Pliny and Plutarch, a hooked grub suspended in a back eddy, his long rod propped up nearby. He is working on a snort of ale and unwrapping some fresh country cheese and biscuits for a snack. He would look with wonder at the ardent, wadered angler of today pushing his way aggressively upstream through the hip-deep flow, covering the holding water with cast after cast, glancing at his wrist watch to see how much time he has left before he must hustle back to the sport utility vehicle and the long drive home.

In the ensuing centuries since Walton fished his English home waters, thousands of books and magazine articles have been published on angling, instructing us on the ever finer points of fishing, especially fishing with flies. We have books about fishing with dry flies, wet flies, nymphs and streamers. Other books guide us to the hot spots on the Yellowstone, Battenkill, Bighorn and the Florida salt flats. We have books that reveal the secrets not only of the various fishes we seek, but the food they eat such as caddisflies, stoneflies, mayflies and baitfish. As in other aspects of our information age, we have more than enough words and pictures on most any aspect of angling. If we could absorb it all, and apply it correctly to the waters we fish, we would all be experts.

We may be better informed anglers today than Walton and his fellow anglers were in seventeenth century England, but we may not be any more "compleat." In many ways we are less complete as anglers today with the undue emphasis on technique and results. The complete angler knows that there is more to fishing than catching fish. Walton knew this and wrote of it first and best. This book is written out of respect and reverence for Walton in the hope of helping in some small way to keep his spirit alive in a world where the many joys of the angling life seem overwhelmed at every turn by endless refinements in method and too little attention to the magic of it all.

To the non-angler all this may seem preposterous, but dedicated anglers will understand. Fishing is about more than catching fish, it is a way of life. It is the north star that orients us. It is a natural way of life in an increasingly unnatural world. It is the motherlode, the touchstone, the bedrock of our being. It allows us to fulfill our predatory instincts that still smolder from the evolutionary fires of our hunter-gatherer past. It grounds us, roots us to who we are and why we are here. And it is more than that.

Some would speculate that this passion to fish fulfills a deep-seated need to connect with the watery element of the world that is the birthplace of life. Without water the land is as lifeless as the mountains of the moon, barren, hard and unforgiving. With water comes life: amino acids, protoplasm, plankton, insects, grasses, trees, fish and mammals. Scientists tell us our distant ancestors crawled out of the water, learned to get their oxygen from air and began the long evolutionary march from fish and reptiles to mammals and man. On an individual basis, we are cocooned in a water world prior to birth, sloshing around in the womb's amniotic fluid, eyes closed and breathing through a tube. To the angler, birth is especially traumatic because it rudely severs us from this watery world and marks the end of our living and breathing in a liquid environment.

Individually and collectively we once lived underwater as do the fishes, but it was only in the beginning of beginnings and

ever since we have inhabited different spheres. We have no conscious memory of our watery ancestry but we nonetheless feel
drawn to our watery roots in ways we cannot comprehend.

What is this fascination with water and with the urge to
communicate with the life of the waters through hook and line?
You could say we are acting out the genetic imprinting of
Homo sapiens, a code of conduct that developed over millions
of years through hunting, fishing and gathering. Agriculture is
little more than 10,000 years old and for more than a million
years prior to that, when our ancestors were developing both
physically and mentally, we fished and hunted in order to survive. That many of us now release our prey unharmed is of no
consequence; the urge that motivates us to pursue these fish—
to stand in cold thigh-deep water or under a blistering sun for
hours and hours hoping for a strike—is to act on this predatory
instinct.

You also could say that we are attracted to fishing because it
is a natural way of life that puts us in touch with the seasons,
with the ebb and flow of the hours and days and months of the
year. Most of our day-to-day world is largely immune from
nature's cycles nowadays as we watch a football game on television that is being played thousands of miles away inside a climate-controlled stadium on artificial turf. Inside shopping malls
the temperature never changes. It never rains and it never
snows and we don't even know if it's day or night. When fishing we are attuned to the seasonal flow of the rivers, the weather, the tides, the cyclical runs of the baitfishes and the game
fishes and the hatch cycles of aquatic insects.

Whatever the cause, we fish because we fish, because the fish
are there and the water is there, just as a mountaineer climbs
mountains because the mountains are there. And while the purpose of fishing is to catch fish, the complete angler knows that
there is more to it than that, just as there is more to love than

sex. To be a complete angler you will want to immerse yourself in the many practical books that instruct you how to read the water, match the hatch, rig your tackle, tie your flies, make the proper presentation, set the hook, play the fish and so forth. Walton provided much practical advice himself, but his instructions were not limited to angling technique alone. As the contemporary bumper sticker says, fishing is not a matter of life and death, it's more important than that.

This book is not about how to catch fish or where to catch fish, but it is about fishing. It is about the other parts of the fishing life that comprise the complete angler. It is about the time we spend thinking fish. It is about fish of memory, fish of the imagination. It is about the friendships that grow with the fishing days, about getting to know your home waters and distant waters, about the food and drink at fishing camp, about fishing truths and fishing lies, about the workings of the natural world, about fishing as youngsters and fishing as old men, about fishing nights in front of the fireplace and how fishing and life are as intertwined as the stands of monofilament in a well-tied blood knot.

# 1. THE SOCIABLE ANGLER

IT IS A GREAT IRONY AND PLEASURE OF THE FISHING LIFE THAT it forges so many strong bonds among friends and family even though fishing is ultimately a solo sport. Fishing doesn't require the participation of others as do many sports and pastimes. You need teammates to play softball. You need partners to play golf. Even other outdoor sports often are group efforts, such as mountain climbing and whitewater rafting.

You can fish alone, and many of us often do, but it's more rewarding to fish with others. When you love something as much as the dedicated angler loves fishing, you want to share that interest with others. Two anglers can talk about the merits of bead-head flies long into the night. You wouldn't even bring up the subject to a non-angler. If you discover the glass bead-heads worked better than the brass bead-heads on a trip, you want to tell someone about it. It is human nature to want to share what is important to you. It would be cold punishment, indeed, for an angler to be marooned in a world of non-anglers, to be unable to talk about his passion, to be rendered mute by others' disinterest.

Fishing has long been a social endeavor since Walton and his companions fished and dined their way across the old English countryside. Being on the water was only part of the fun for Walton's characters who filled country inns with poetry and laughter and who sought out the sweet-voiced milkmaids for song after a good day's fishing.

"Good company makes the way seem short," is Walton's testament to the pleasure of companionship on the fishing waters.

Good fishing company begins for many anglers with their fathers who introduced them to the angling life. Father may have been a serious angler or not so serious, but for many of us the earliest memories of the angling waters are with dad. At first he rigged your tackle, cast the bait into the pond and handed you the rod. When the fish came to the net, he brought it in and killed it with a quick blow to the head with a rusty pair of pliers. Later, he taught you how to tie a cinch knot, thread on a night crawler, pinch on the split-shot. He showed you where to fish, how to fish and when to fish. He may have even tried to explain why we fish, but that can take time, and it is an introspective subject even many adults ignore. There's the story, it may even be true, of the gruff fishing magazine editor who admonished a dewy-eyed writer to stick to the how-to and where-to stories and not worry about the why.

"Our readers already know why they fish," the editor said.

Dad may not have said a word about why he fished, and why he wanted to teach you to fish, but you got the picture. He fished because it was fun, because it allowed him to leave the world of work and care behind and come close to another world, one without deadlines, except the coming of darkness at the end of the day. You sensed that fishing was something that excited him and that transformed him from dad the provider to dad the guy with the long rod and funny hat, focused on hooking odd looking, dim-witted, slimy creatures. You saw a new intensity in dad's eyes when on the water. You sensed that he knew a fair amount about this arcane world of rod and reel, fish and flies, worms and rooster tails. Fishing with dad was about more than catching fish; it was about seeing him in a different way, about adding another dimension to this perplexing, dominating force in your life. Fishing is a great leveler, whether among adults or between adults and children. When you are fishing everyone is equal: the Denver carpenter alongside the Silicon Valley executive. The fish don't distinguish between the Elk Hair Caddis offered by one and the Elk Hair Caddis offered by the other. For the child, and the dad, too, fishing levels the terrain. A fishing trip is a welcome truce between parent and child: no expectations, no scolding, no nagging. You are in it together and you are more equal than at home.

"You're equaler," as a child might say. The fishing waters have a way of eroding the berm that separates the grown from the growing. Despite the child's lack of fishing experience, there is no assurance that his or her angling efforts will go any more unrewarded than those of the more experienced father. When you are both trolling F-4 Flatfish behind the boat with an ounce of lead on each rig, things are about as equitable as they can get. The fish don't care whose hand is on the cork.

Whether you are a dad or a child this democracy on the water is refreshing. When I've gone in search of fish with my children, I have felt a commonality of purpose that we don't always share otherwise, each of us channeled into our modern-day division of labor. I imagine that in what we call the more primitive societies, the difference between children and adults is not what it is in our society. Sure the children are smaller in stature, but they are enmeshed in the same activities as the adults. You spear fish together, hunt deer together and gather roots and berries together. You get better at these tasks as you grow and gain experience, but the world of adult work and worries is not the great unknown that it is for children today. Today's schoolhouse is a long way from the sterile clean rooms of the computer chip manufacturers or the rarified offices in tall skyscrapers. We train our young in places that most adults seldom return to after they grow up, and we adults work in places that are too specialized, too dangerous or too boring for children to survive.

On the angling waters this is not so. Adult and child are united in their pursuit of a common quarry. Dad may go about it more methodically than the child, but when the rod tip quivers and then throbs with a fish on the line he is as excited as the six-year-old beside him. Youth and adult find common ground on the angling waters. At home, common turf is not as easy to find as dad quickly tires of playing dolls and many other children's games. And the kids are not very interested in dad's books or music or chess or conversations with mom about incomprehensible subjects. But on the angling waters, both are focused with equal interest on the catching of fish. Whether this means the child rises in stature to a higher level when fishing, or whether this means the father descends to a child's level, is open for debate. There are those who would argue the latter, but the reality is that the dad and child are joined together in common purpose.

The common experience of family angling builds family traditions, too. We look back upon our parents and grandparents and into the future through our children and their children and establish our lineage, our mark on the earth, inconsequential though it might be in the cosmic march of time. This is who I am, this family tree, and it grounds me, roots me to others blooded as I am and to the land where we live. To have fished with your predecessors and your progeny and their progeny is to enliven this lineage, invest it with a shared sense of purpose that transcends generations and stills time.

Once, years ago, my wife and I and our first child made a trip to Montana to camp, fish and visit my father's hometown and home waters. An inquiry at a Missoula cemetery lead us to several generations of Alkire gravestones: the paternal grandfather I never met and his father, too, their remains resting underfoot, one with the Montana earth that sustained them in the late nineteenth century and the early years of the twentieth century. My young son and I are in the photo in front of those two gravestones, and except for the absence of my father, then in his late sixties and not along on the trip, we were five generations at once.

We camped not far away on Rock Creek, a well-known western Montana trout stream. On the first evening I fished upstream from camp and stumbled into a number of trout that were interested in the Humpy patterns I had brought along for these Montana waters. These high-floating dry flies perched on the film and drifted into pods of working fish which seemed to think the Humpy resembled some type of natural born insect, though I have no idea what that insect might have been. My son fished with a short, closed bail spin rod and reel using a bubble float with a Humpy attached onto it in the shallow water near camp. It was a fine summertime Montana camp with only a few other parties in the campground. The morning hikes in the nearby hills had that edge to them that you only get when hiking in country that might have grizzly bears about. Foolishly perhaps, I didn't bother carrying a firearm, but we did make a lot of intentional noise, which is not difficult to do with a three-year-old child along. There were the predictable summer afternoon thunderstorms of the Rockies where the sky darkens sometime after lunch and the air seems to change its electrical charge. There's a change in the elements that you can smell and see. Then you hear a low rumbling noise high up in the snow-clawed mountaintops and then comes the rain, sudden, hard and brief. You take cover for twenty minutes and then the clouds disappear, blown away over to the Clark Fork Valley, or over the top of the Sapphire Mountains, or back up against the Anaconda Range. The sun reappears and shines brightly on the pine needles and underbrush that is thinly splattered with rain, evaporating quickly in the dry, high-altitude air. And in the evening the bats emerge and chase your fly on the false cast as it blurs with the night hatches that cloud the river with trout food. The summer twilight, long in these northern latitudes, lingers into the bedtime hour and campfire time is brief, but still long enough for roasted marshmallows.

And as I lay in the sleeping bag warding off the quickening chill that is part of this country even in mid-summer, I think of this river many decades ago when my dad was learning to fish these waters: hellgrammites plucked from the streamside rocks, Royal Coachman attractor patterns, catgut leaders. Much was the same then as with my son and me now, and some things were different. There was the threading of the leader through the eye of the hook, tying a good improved cinch knot, reading the water, casting to a likely spot. Of course, that was before the National Fly-Fishing Act of 1992, the year actor Brad Pitt played a gifted but doomed young Montana fly angler in the movie, *A River Runs Through It*. Back then, in the old days, there were no graphite rods, no neoprene waders with Velcro suspender snaps. A sport utility vehicle was your uncle's battered Model T Ford flecked with fish scales and elk blood. Back then, there was at least one three-piece bamboo fly rod in the Alkire angling arsenal that I know of for I have used it as an adult. And there were other rods and reels, leader wallets and flies lost over the decades that once were used to catch fish on this chattering trout stream that looked much the same in the days between the wars as it looks today. The trout were different then and they were the same, here by an act of God or by the accidents of evolution or by whatever reason you ascribe to the presence of beauty in the world. And while the fish were really not the same fish and the water really not the same water of fifty years ago, the big river rocks and even some of the big yellow belly Ponderosa pines may have been the same ones my forebears saw. The steep hillsides draining the snowmelt into the rivulets and tributary creeks have been virtually unchanged in that short span of geologic time. Down on the river I like to imagine that some of the bridges spanning the little tributaries that we crossed in the old Chevrolet station wagon were some of the ones constructed by my grandfather who built bridges for the Forest Service in that area. But this is wishful thinking as those early-day wooden bridges probably did not last a half a century. Years of spring floods probably took care of them; roiling muddy water pushing windfalls into bridge abutments, angry cascades of snowmelt oblivious to the works of man, intent only on moving toward the sea more than one thousand miles away.

I have my own home water and it is not in Montana, but it is good to know of my family's home water even if I never fish it again. I feel more centered, as the mystics say about such things, after having been on this ancestral home water. Its waters eventually flow into the Columbia River and therefore commingle with the waters of my home water, which also drains into the Columbia, as does most of the interior Pacific Northwest. I'm glad for this accident of genealogy and geology, for if my grandfather had settled east of the Great Divide, where he met my grandmother on the windswept plains of central Montana, his home waters might have flowed east instead of west. Our waters then would have never entwined; they would have flowed into different oceans. For a westerner, the Gulf of Mexico, the Caribbean Sea, the Atlantic Ocean all seem far away. I consider myself fortunate, more absolutely centered, nearly plumb centered, that the Alkire waters, old and new, flow to the ocean as one plume. Of course, if I trace the family tree further back, the source and identity of the family home waters become more obscure: before Montana there was Missouri, and before that Virginia, and before that somewhere along the German-Dutch border and so on. Family ties unravel when stretched beyond the reach of those we have known personally. During our four-score and ten years most of us are lucky to know one or two generations on either side of our own, the blood unit of time most meaningful to us. Distant relations are as distant waters, fine perhaps but far away from our everyday lives.

Fishing binds us to family and it binds us to non-kin too, forging some of life's most endearing friendships. The circle of people you get to know through a lifetime's fishing is like the rise rings of a surface-feeding fish, concentric circles rippling across the water's skin. At the epicenter of the rise are those whom you actually spend time with on the water: fishing, camping, traveling together. Beyond that are many other friends whom you talk to about fishing, but seldom accompany on a fishing trip. This is not because you don't want to fish with them, but because there is so little time in most of our schedules to get out on the water and much more time to talk about it. I'm not sure if other endeavors result in as much chatter time as fishing, but anglers are great talkers. Go to a party and two anglers will discover one another and proceed to ignore everyone else in the room for the next hour while they exchange fishing stories. This may be more of an urban phenomenon, for I'm told that rural anglers who live close to the fishing waters and actually number their annual fishing days into the triple digits don't bother as much with the fishing clubs, sportsmen's shows, fly-tying demonstrations, fishing books and magazines and so forth. They are living the fishing life full time and don't need to participate in it vicariously, as do the rest of us.

For those of us who don't live a ten-minute walk from good fishing water and who don't number our annual fishing days in the triple digits, fish talk is important. It seems as though I spend as much time talking about fishing with friends whom I've never or seldom fished with as I do talking with my regular fishing partners. For one thing, there is an instant familiarity with others who fish, especially if you are both fly anglers. You appreciate the same challenge of the quest, the thrill of the take, the excitement that comes with a large fish running downstream on a light line filling the quiet river morning with the high-pitched mechanical whirling sound of double tapered line spooling off the reel. In a room full of serious anglers you've likely found a congregation that shares a similar catechism: minimize the hours spent in search of economic sustenance; maximize the hours on the water; minimize the time spent re-grouting bathroom tile or repairing the screen door; concoct family vacations that include time on fishable waters; spend your precious spare time on the banks of a river instead of on the couch in front of the television.

Once not so very long ago, before fly fishing became the national pastime de rigueur, fly anglers were largely a bumbling, eccentric lot of misfits who poked around the edges of streams and rivers wearing floppy hats, baggy waders and puffing away on briarwood pipes. In those days there was a saying: "There are no strangers in the fly fishing fraternity, only friends we haven't met." I always liked that adage, even though it wasn't always true then and has even less the ring of truth today.

Still, there is a certain core truth to it that those who are awe-struck by the power, mystery and thrill of the angle are brothers of the angle, too, as Walton said. Part of this closeness with others who fish lies in a shared interest, in finding others whom you can talk to about fly patterns, wading boots, common waters and new tactics. But part of it too is that this common interest culls out those with less desirable personality traits. You are less likely to encounter truly obnoxious people on the fishing waters than elsewhere. Everyone who wears a fishing vest will not end up being your best friend, but you will find fewer jerks among anglers than you will in the general population. This is not to say that jerks never invade the angling waters; they do, even in the rarified world of fly fishing. I've seen them and so have you: the guys who barge into the water you are fishing uninvited, without even a salutation; the guys who confuse guides with valets; the hole hogs who homestead a good piece of public water as though they carry title to it.

And then you must deal with the guys who have taken a Stalinist approach to the catch-and-release fly fishing ethic, the ones who consider you a knuckle-dragging Cro-Magnon if you kill a fish every so often where the rules allow a limited take. I remember one anal-retentive priss who admonished me for equipping my five-year-old daughter with a small pink spin rod and reel on a piece of water restricted to fly tackle only. With that equipment she was able to cast a bubble and fly a few feet out into the stream and thereby fish alongside her brother and me who were both using fly gear. While technically illegal, the threat to the fish was zero given her angling ability, and I considered this a small bending of the rules that even a game warden would have winked at.

"This is fly rod-only-water, you know," the priss told me as we walked by him on the bank of the river. I was taken up short by his comment and stopped.

"Yea, I know," I said glaring at him. I had to remind myself of my angling manners and not run the tip of my eight-foot graphite rod up his nasal passage or down his throat. We walked by him, but I remained steamed for hours. I still am. Why if I ever come across that fly fishing Gestapo geek I'll break his neck, I'll ... So much for the brotherhood of fly fishermen.

Despite such exceptions, there remains an easy-going familiarity among anglers, fly fishermen in particular, where you can walk into a fly shop in Bozeman, Redding, Key West, St. Louis or Manchester and talk the talk. And even the insensitive angler may not be beyond redemption. Often these anglers violate angling decorum out of ignorance, not always because they are natural born butts. Some younger anglers, for example, who did not have a father or uncle to guide them in their formative fishing years, do not actually realize they are being rude when they splash into "your" water. Or maybe, the offender hails from a densely populated area of the country where people are accustomed to fishing shoulder to shoulder, just as they are accustomed to being squeezed cheek to cheek into subway cars or into high-rise office elevators. I can recall the shock I felt years ago on a trip to Europe when my wife and I were herded, shoved like livestock, into a train car on a trip through Portugal. Like animals, people get accustomed to how they are treated; they adapt to survive. If I had spent twenty years in Portugal then I'd probably elbow my neighbor into a packed train car, too. Let these people loose on a sparsely populated Oregon river, and they probably don't realize that they are violating anyone's space as they step into the river twenty yards downstream of your fishing station.

But this is about the sociable angler, not the insensitive angler, and most of the anglers I have socialized with over the years have been a good bunch. Some whom I have met have become good friends while others, whom I initially knew outside of the fishing world, have become even better friends through our shared interest in angling. And then there are the people you meet on angling trips, in fly shops, restaurants, camp grounds and on the water whom you never see again but who make an impression on you and enrich your life. On a trip not long ago with my California friend, Bill, on the upper Sacramento River, we fished with little success for a day and a half in the river's deep canyon. On the afternoon of the second day we left camp and drove into Dunsmuir to Ted Fay's Fly Shop, a local institution suspended in time, named after a pioneering fly angler of the northern California waters. The shop was, at least back then in the mid-1990s, housed in a very small old wooden building in front of an equally old motel shaded by tall pine trees. If you are old enough, this was the kind of motel your family stayed in on road trips to out-of-the-way places in the 1950s and 1960s. It was an irony that this vintage fly shop was located in the densely populated, trend setting state of California, in contrast to the large well-lighted, stylish fly shops that you find in many of the other western states far removed from the centers of style.

Inside, there were no English waxed cotton jackets on display. In fact, there was little clothing at all for sale. Unlike so many of our fly-fishing shops nowadays, this one was still a fishing store, not a clothing store. There were no expensive fold-up wading staffs either; instead there were some locally made wooden staffs, selling for a very reasonable price. Behind the counter was the slumped, frail figure of an old man, nodding off in the afternoon warmth. His hair was gray and short clipped, and his face was well wrinkled. If he was younger than 70 years old I'd be surprised. Bill and I nosed around the shop at the gear and the photos on the wall. It was as small a fishing shop as I had seen in some time. You could touch every corner of the store by standing in the center and waving an eight-foot rod around. Gradually, the old guy behind the counter came to life and we told him where we were fishing.

"I don't want to offend you, but if you've been fishing nymphs the usual way you didn't catch any fish, did you?" asked the old guy, whose name we later learned was Joe.

"No, it's been pretty slow," I said, struck by his clairvoyance, as we had said nothing yet about our lack of success on the water.

"It's not slick water here," Joe said, referring to the tumultuous pocket water in the narrow canyon. He cleared his throat and rose from the stool he had been sitting on. He seemed taller than I had expected and his face now had less the ashen look of a tired old man. He explained to us that we should fish a short line: two or three feet of fly line and a seven-and-one-half-foot leader with the upper end colored for visibility. You have to wade in close to the pocket water you're fishing and keep that line short, he said. The more he talked the more animated he became. His voice deepened and quickened and he stepped out from behind the counter and grabbed an old bait-fishing rod with a fly reel attached to it. He made an imaginary cast toward the corner of the room about three feet away.

"If it's further than that, it's TOO far," Joe said loudly, instructing us on the merits of fishing close in and tight. He told us how to keep your rod tip up during the drift of the nymph.

"High sticking," Joe said. Use a split shot above the nymph and watch the curl in your leader. When you see the slightest movement, set the hook, he said. By now his voice was booming, and with Bill's ever-loud voice chiming in too, the small shop was bursting with volume. Almost dancing on his toes and still holding the rod, Joe slid up to Bill and grabbed his arm and shook it.

"When you feel the strike, it's too late. Got to see the leader move," Joe shouted, making his point in words and in deed. Bill rocked back in place as Joe removed his hand from Bill's arm.

Bill and I both nodded and repeated the refrain: "When you feel the strike, it's too late."

"How about using a strike indicator?" I asked meekly, awed by the volcanic awakening of this old guy whose pants were held up by fish-print suspenders. None of the testosterone impaired help at the fancy Rocky Mountain fly shops could hold a candle to this veteran who had at first seemed one step removed from the grave. He was not only telling us what to use and how to fish, but was giving us a full-bodied, red-blooded demonstration.

"Nope, never use them," Joe said in response to my query about using strike indicators, almost the norm at the time for fishing nymphs on most trout rivers. By the time the indicator moves, it's too late, he said. Just watch the colored end of the leader. You can paint your leaders with fingernail polish, Joe said. Or you can buy leaders with the upper end already pre-painted, he added.

Joe put away the rod, stepped behind the counter and settled back onto his wooden stool. His chest seemed to contract a little, his face lost some of its swollen redness and his voice softened. Still, he sat erect and alert behind the glass and wood counter, firmly in command of his angling ship wedged into the narrow canyon of the upper Sacramento, a river once thick with large chinook salmon, its ice-cold tributaries once the southern limit of the environmentally sensitive bull trout. We discussed fly patterns and purchased a dozen or so including some of the late Ted Fay's Bomber series, plus we purchased some of the colored leaders that he had in stock. On the way out Joe wished us good luck and directed us to the small black chalkboard propped against the outside of the shop with the latest information on the local hatches. You could come by the shop anytime, day or night, and check out the board, he said.

If you fish long enough you will be lucky to meet anglers such as Joe, the bedrock of angling society. It is one of the pleasures of the fishing life that you encounter such people, dedicated to their way of life, sure of their purpose and willing to share with others.

Another pleasure of the fishing life is the friendships that grow over the years with your fishing partners, the handful of people within your larger angling circle whom you actually fish with on a regular basis. I've been fortunate to have a number of good fishing partners: some I've known since grade school, others less than a decade. Partner is a good word for a fishing companion as it denotes more than friendship, it means you are joined in a common activity. Of course, there are many different types of partners from business partners to domestic partners, but to me the most genuine use of the word applies to outdoor partners in the western context of partnering prospectors and cowboys.

> My foot's in the stirrup,
> My pony won't stand;
> Goodbye, old partner,
> I'm leaving Cheyenne.

(Preface to *Leaving Cheyenne* by Larry McMurtry, 1963)

The main link between fishing partners is not economic as in business partners, although sometimes economics does play a minor role. For example, I'm linked economically to several fishing partners through mutual outdoor interests: I co-own a drift boat with one partner; I co-own a bird dog with another partner; and I co-own a bag of goose decoys with yet another partner. You could call me a half-assed sportsman if you want with half a boat and half a dog, but that's been my way of financing some of the accoutrements of the outdoor life.

Selecting your fishing partners is not a matter to be taken lightly. Spending time on the water with a good partner is always a pleasure; fish for a day with a jerk and it is a long day, indeed. There are certain personality characteristics that you seek and others that you may want to avoid in a good fishing partner. Call it the art and science of partnering, if you will, even though it is much more art than science. The first step in partnering is to avoid the competitive guys: fishing is a non-competitive sport. If you want to compete, play golf. Play tennis. Play softball. Don't fish. There's no room on the fishing waters for competition, and you certainly want to avoid fishing with someone whose goal is to catch more fish than you. Our modern-day culture oozes competition and fishing is one way of getting away from this unfortunate fact of life. The lack of competition is one of fishing's most noteworthy characteristics. There is no winner or loser, no scorekeeper, no playoffs. It's you and the water and the fish and that's it. Fishing is more meaningful to us than many other things we do precisely because it is not competitive. It is more like life—real life—which is not a game at all, where the only winner is time, which defeats us all in the end. When you fish you measure yourself against the mysteries and whims of nature; you match your skill against the fish and not your fellow fishermen.

We all know there are anglers who bring along the competitive spirit from the business world and the sports world to the fishing waters, and it may be unfair to be prejudiced against such competitive persons. Maybe they can't help themselves. Some well-known anglers over the years have been openly competitive. By his own, and others' accounts, Ernest Hemingway was a very competitive angler, bent as he was on catching record-book marlin in the Caribbean's bluewater fishery.

Consider the harsh words that Arnold Gingrich, founding editor of *Esquire* and an enthusiastic angler, had for Hemingway after fishing with him out of Key West in the mid-1930s. "He [Hemingway] was also—and this is what no true angler is—intensely competitive about his fishing, and a very poor sport," Gingrich said in his book, *The Well-Tempered Angler.* "If the luck was out, then nobody around him could do any right, and he was ready to blame everybody in sight, ahead of himself. When things were going right, he was quick to promote everybody in his company to high rank as good fellows, and was jovially boastful about their every least accomplishment, as well as his own," he wrote. As an angler, something seemed to happen to Hemingway as he grew from the youthful Midwest trout fisherman in the *Big Two-Hearted River* to the competitive deep-sea angler of his later years. I would have liked to have been along for the trout, but I'm not so sure about the marlin.

A good fishing partner will not compete against you on the waters but will take pleasure in your successes and help you if the fish don't cooperate. If your partner is catching all the fish and you are not, he will share his success with you, let you know where the fish are biting and what they are taking. And if the tables are turned and you are the one catching the fish, a good partner will not get in too deep a funk about it all. He will enjoy the fishing regardless of whether the catching is good or not. He will approach his fishing with intensity, but with an understanding too that sometimes the fish don't cooperate. This, of course, is easier said than done. I can recall a number of fishing trips when I've struggled with disappointment at not hooking the number or size of fish that I had hoped to hook. But this disappointment will pass and you have to learn how to put it in perspective. The competitive sports are filled with as much disappointment as glory, and the good players know how to sleep off defeat and face the next game with fresh enthusiasm.

Usually, but not always, fishing partners tend to be of similar age—within ten years of one another. There are many exceptions, and it would be nice if there were more, but like other friendships, those forged on the water also are more easily cemented between those going through similar stages of life. The father of a newborn likely has more in common with another new father than with a fishing partner with five grandchildren. Similar physical abilities tie together partners too, dictate how far you can hike, how aggressively you can wade. When you want to complain about how difficult it is to tie on a size 20 midge pattern, your words will elicit a different understanding from a fifty-year-old partner than from a thirty-year-old partner.

A good partner will usually offer you the choice of what water to fish when you arrive at a likely spot. And you hope that you always make such an offer in turn. Again, this is not always easy to do, especially, if you arrive at a spot and there is a familiar riffle where you have caught fish before and you want to wade right in. But your partner might be thinking the same thing. A good partner will anticipate the direction you are fishing and will not cut in front of you. He will always ask first if there is any question. If you're on a small stream, a good partner will make sure the two of you don't crowd the water. As one fisherman I know says, two anglers fishing a small piece of water is like two guys making love to the same woman, it can be done but it's not very satisfying. Once you have fished with someone for awhile, all this will be automatic. You will learn the type of water your partner prefers, the way he likes to fish, how long he stays in any one stretch of water, how far he wanders off and so on. With a long-time partner there is no awkwardness.

There is some debate on whether a partner should be a more or less accomplished angler than you. It works both ways. You learn something every trip from a more accomplished partner, but you run the risk of despondency if he always catches more fish than you do. Then again, maybe you should pay closer attention to your angling efforts if this pattern persists. One of my best fishing partners is a much better angler than me and always will be and it doesn't bother me at all. I am honored to fish with him. He is always helpful and never boastful when he is successful and I am not. I wish I could be the angler he is, but I recognized years ago that some of us are more natural born anglers than others, just as some of us are more natural born athletes than others. Some anglers seem to know intuitively what the fish are taking and where and when. You watch them and they have a way of absorbing all the conditions—the water conditions, hatches, light, weather—and formulating a strategy that actually works. If God didn't endow you with this intuition, may you have the good fortune to partner with someone who has such abilities.

The list of the qualities of a good fishing partner could go on and on: sense of humor, willingness to help with camp chores, adaptability to changing conditions, no whining, no holy rollers and no snoring in the tent. But a list is only a list and good partners are more than the sum of so many attributes. There is a chemistry, more an alchemy really, among anglers that when it works generates not only a comfortable, congenial camp but at times a mapcap hilarity as well. And at times an angling camp can border on the absurd, such as the time not long ago when I met a few fishing friends, some whom I knew well and others whom I did not, on a river not too far away. The fishing conditions were not good on this particular June weekend, as the water level was too high. The river was running in tight and deep under the streamside alders making wading difficult. The rain came down in fits and starts all day long. And the wind kicked up too periodically.

While such conditions might have discouraged many anglers, still most of us might have at least tried a few casts. Not this group. Perhaps there were too many anglers in the same camp who knew one another and the social magnetism was simply overwhelming. Or, perhaps the conditions really were too adverse. But even I was surprised by the number of anglers who didn't even bother uncasing their rods: metal and plastic tubes with fine graphite rods, carefully packed and buried in the back of cars, remained untouched for two days. Their owners were so busy talking fishing that they forgot to fish: a bunch of middle-aged guys sitting around in folding camp chairs, talking non-stop for hours about fishing while one of the West's premier trout rivers flowed by in front of them unfished.

I consider myself somewhat of a bullshitter, but in this case I shut up and listened to the experts. Every now and again a guy would brave the elements and fish awhile. When he returned, usually with little success to report, it simply added fuel to the fire of the camp anglers. These guys couldn't be bothered with the river at their front door when they had rivers of memories to rely upon. They were too busy showing each other photographs of their Caribbean bonefishing trips: long narratives accompanied the pictures, of course.

"And here's the dock where we met the guide in the morning," said one of the bonefishing experts as he pointed to a photograph. When in the Bahamas or Belize or on Christmas Island these guys probably show one another pictures of their Pacific Northwest fishing trips while resting under the shade of a beach umbrella.

"And here's the backeddie where I hooked the twenty-inch rainbow...Another margarita, senorita," I can hear them say.

I number these anglers among my friends, and I relate this story not out of disrespect, but to illustrate what good fishing chemistry can produce: fishing partners who are too busy partnering to fish. Some would say this is in keeping with the Zen of fishing, where the angler lapses into trance-like meditation while covering the big waters with cast after cast. In the instance of the uncased rods, the anglers moved onto a higher level of angling awareness, free from the pesky conditions of the actual riverine environment, cumbersome waders and bothersome casting. They were beyond the physical and into the metaphysical. They were on the Platonic plane contemplating the distilled essence of angling, the idea of fishing independent of its physical reality. Deep angling. Angling beyond angling.

Does this nonsense happen in other endeavors? I doubt it. Golfers retire to the nineteenth hole after playing the first eighteen holes; they don't start out there and finish up there eight hours later. Or maybe they do and I haven't heard about it. But in fishing it can happen and does. The social bonds can overwhelm the very reason for the adventure, a strange turn of events for what is considered a solo sport.

# II. The Well-Traveled Angler

ONE OF THE PLEASURES OF THE ANGLING LIFE IS EXPLORING new waters. No matter how wedded an angler is to his home river, lake, bay or inlet, it is rare for him not to stray and fish more distant waters from time to time. Call it the angling wanderlust, but few fishermen are immune from it. Fish are virtually omnipresent in the world and somewhere there are more fish, larger fish, stronger fighting fish just waiting for you: rainbows in Montana, browns in New Zealand, peacock bass in Amazon tributaries, kings on the Kenai, bones in Barbados, and tarpon in Key West. The angling addict gets excited just thinking about all the possibilities. In a lifetime of fishing you could never do it all.

But the traveling angler should be cautious, for fishing far-off can be full of hazards, not the least being your own overly grand expectations. It is not surprising that anglers develop unrealistic expectations about their pending trips given the tremendous promotion of fishing destinations by outdoor magazines, sporting shows and the tourist industry. The hype is unrelenting and the fireside angler relaxing in his easy chair on a cold January evening dreaming of an exotic fishing trip is easy prey. The promotional focus is always on the most successful moments of a trip, the cheerful sunny days, the days when the fish are feeding fools ready to snap at whatever you offer. The more distant the destination and the more expensive the trip, the greater the expectation. An auto trip to a neighboring state to camp and fish on a new piece of water does not raise expectations, as does a $1,000 per day trip to Chile.

The raw angling truth is that you can have bad fishing days in Belize as easily as in Missouri. You can find bad weather and unwilling fish halfway around the world or close to home. You may not encounter such bad luck; everything may be tip-top on your trip, but then again it may not. I remember meeting a disappointed young couple from the lower 48 on a river in central Alaska some years ago. The lodge that they had booked a trip through had called them and said the silvers were in and they had better come a week earlier than they had originally planned. The couple made the necessary arrangements at work and home to leave early and flew north with great expectations. They arrived at the lodge via floatplane and after a day on the water found out that the silvers were not in the river yet. It was choked with pinks, smaller, finely scaled salmon that like sockeye offer little sport once in fresh water. You could snag them if you wanted and horse them around, but it wasn't really fishing. The male pinks' backs were humped, giving them their nickname "humpies," and their jaws were distended and "hooked" by the approaching rigors of spawning. They had no interest in chasing a fly or spoon. Closer to salt water they offered great sport, but not here. Many Alaskans distain pinks and claim that even the bears won't eat them. My companions and I discovered the same disappointing truth about the absence of silvers, but we were there for only an overnight drop camp at little expense. The young Idaho couple was stuck for a week. And the day before their guide had gone off on a drunk and had not been seen since. You only hear about such angling disappointments through personal experience or friends; you won't read about the dark side of the travel business in the travel section of your daily newspaper or in the outdoor magazines.

The traveling angler needs to be realistic and cautious. At the same time, he doesn't want to be anal-retentive. Travel, real travel, is about venturing into the unknown, whether it is angling or non-angling travel. You don't want to be ripped off by an unscrupulous outfitter, but then again you don't want every hour of every day planned out six months in advance. The traveling angler even more so than the ordinary traveler enters a world largely beyond his control because you never know what the fish and weather will do: sometimes the fish are simply not there; sometimes the bite is off; sometimes the weather keeps you off the water. Even with the most thorough planning, angling is always an adventure beyond the control of the best guides. You wouldn't want it otherwise or it wouldn't be fishing. If you want a sure thing, go to a well-stocked trout pond. Real fishing entails dealing with a hundred variables, most of which you have no control over. The accomplished angler learns how to adapt to such changing conditions. And he knows that the fishing cannot always be good. He learns to enjoy the traveling in addition to the fishing, especially at times when the fishing is disappointing: he enjoys new surroundings, new people, new customs, a different landscape, a different architecture. After all, the angling wanderlust is motivated not simply by the desire to catch a lot of large fish, but to explore new country. Many anglers are restless explorers at heart and fishing seems only an excuse to enter new territory. Fishing provides a focus, a wedge into the life of a new country.

Fishing brought me to Alaska once, but I took back more than the memories of the fish caught, more than an ice chest packed with salmon and halibut fillets. Chasing fish from Prince William Sound to the rivers of Cook Inlet reveals to the traveling angler a varied landscape of monumental proportions. You discover immense tidal flats that give way to thin forests of skinny conifers growing part way up the mountain slopes to the tree line. In other areas you find mountains that rise straight out of the sea, no tidal flats at all, just the salt and then the mountains cut with glaciers still calving their ancient ice into the bay. You see a bull moose run across the road entering the Anchorage International Airport. You stop at a bridge spanning Quartz Creek and look at the mass of sock-eye: bank to bank, nose to tail, side by side, glazed dark eyes, slowly dying, heads green, bodies red, all in a mindless quest to reach their spawning grounds, instinct urging them on to procreate and then die.

You feel a profound tiredness after several days in the far north where you can fish until midnight and start all over again a few hours later at dawn. You begin to grasp the psychological roller coaster that those living near the Arctic Circle ride year in and year out as they adjust to the waxing and waning daylight. It would be a depressing place in the winter with dawn arriving just before the lunch hour and dusk shortly thereafter. In the summer it is an exuberant place with the nearly endless sunshine, but you would have to temper your activities with your body's need for rest. After a few days I too acclimated and learned to go to bed with the sun still in the sky.

It is the patient angler who appreciates both the travel and the angling when on a long-distance fishing trip. He understands that the fishing is only part of a fishing trip. And patience is a much needed attribute when fishing away from home for when the fishing is slow in a strange land it seems slower than on a slow day at home. This probably has to do with the overly high expectations that so often accompany exotic fishing trips. A slow day on your home waters is a disappointment, but you will be back next week or next month and the month after that and next year and the year after that and so on. Not so with your much anticipated trip to Costa Rica where you have invested a great deal of money into five fun-filled days and now the wind is gusting at 20 knots for the third day in a row keeping you off the prime fishing water. And then when you do get on the water the fish are not to be found. Bad weather days, days when the bite is off, sick days, all these off-the-mark days are more keenly felt when you have traveled far with high hopes.

Even if the fishing is fair, you still may be disappointed due to the great expectations you had for the trip. A twelve-inch brookie on your home waters in Vermont pleases you, but on a Montana trout stream, where you expect much more, a twelve-incher is nothing. It takes time away from casting for the really big boys, the ones that you traveled so far to hook. When you boarded the plane your expectations changed. You raised the bar, and now your catches will have to be larger and more numerous to prove satisfactory. I am not ashamed to admit that I have been skunked a number of times at home and away, but those times away have been more painful. When you think about it, this is the reverse of how it should be. On my home water I should know the lies, know the flies, know the secrets of the place. It should hurt more, not less to come away fishless at the end of the day. Away from home you are fishing for a different type of fish in different water that is completely foreign to you so why shouldn't you get skunked?

Grand expectations that accompany fishing in far-off places also can warp fishing's underlying principal—context. All angling is within context. Hooking eight-inch brookies on a two-weight rod in a creek you can jump across can be as thrilling as battling marlin more than double your own weight in the bluewater fishery. In between is all manner of angling that we all adapt to given our home bases and individual proclivities. Hooking a ten-inch trout while deep trolling a Ford Fender in a mountain lake is not the same as hooking it in a small creek with light gear. I often experience this fishing relativity on my home water where I fish for both trout and steelhead. During the spring, when there are no steelhead in the river, a fifteen-inch rainbow is a delight and an eighteen-incher on the line makes your day. In the early fall when the steelhead are running and you are fishing for this much larger fish, an accidentally hooked fifteen-inch trout suddenly is not the joy it once was a few months earlier.

When you write your four-figure check to cover the cost of a far-off fishing trip you subconsciously lose interest in smaller fish or smaller quantities of fish. You up the ante. You want the big guys and plenty of them. The context is changed and so are your expectations. Unconsciously, you set yourself up for disappointment on such trips by these upwardly creeping expectations that are reinforced at every turn by the magazines, books, outfitters, lodges and fishing shops. The truly wise well-traveled angler is enthusiastic about his next adventure, but guards against overly grand expectations. He keeps in touch with his inner Buddhist self that tells him desire is the root of all suffering. Eliminate desire and you eliminate suffering.

Well, you don't want to go so far as to eliminate all desire, for you don't want to lose your desire to fish. Hold onto that desire, the angling passion that defines you, but resist the temptation of unrealistic expectations. Excitement is good, expectations are dangerous. It is a wonderful thing to travel, to see new country, to meet new people and fish for new fish, but the thoughtful angler will come away with finer memories of his trips if he embarks on his journey wearing untinted glasses.

The traveling angler will have a better trip too if he or she approaches his adventure with openness. Don't be too particular about the type of fish you want to catch, the type of waters you want to fish and your choice of tackle. Several long-distance trips I have taken were deeply enriched by abandoning my pre-trip notions of exactly what I wanted to fish for and how I wanted to fish. On my first venture into sub-tropical angling I had visions of wading the flats and fly fishing for snook and redfish. This came to pass, and it was a great pleasure to hook a hard-fighting snook under a hot Florida sun using a fly that I had tied months before in the depths of a cold, wet Oregon winter. It was a revelation for a western angler accustomed to cold wading water, even in summer, to wade in the bathtub-warm water of Tampa Bay, Sarasota Bay, Terra Ceia Bay. No waders were required, just a swimsuit, a thin cotton long-sleeved shirt and a broad-brimmed hat. It was so simple. You didn't need your felt-soled, metal-studded wading boots to grip a rocky, slippery stream bottom. You just pulled on a pair of rubber water socks and shuffled along in the soft sand.

This new experience was rewarding, but the best part of the trip came after I hung up my fly rod and wading socks. Usually, I prefer to fish with fly gear and I prefer to wade rather than fish out of a boat. There's no snobbishness intended here, just personal angling preference. Too much is made of fly fishing these days and it can generate an unfortunate attitude on the part of some of its adherents. A fisherman who has never used any gear but fly gear is missing something in his angling evolution. The Complete Angler knows how to thread a worm on a hook just as he knows how to present a Parachute Adams into a feeding lane. I have threaded a good many small creatures onto hooks: worms, grasshoppers, crayfish, shrimp and herring, as well as gobs of sticky, smelly salmon roe. Still, I prefer using a fly rod and reel with artificial flies and that's what I had wanted to do on this southern saltwater trip. I wanted to catch hard-fighting game fish on light tackle, in shallow water and on flies.

However, we had heard that tarpon were running just off-shore, south of Tampa Bay along the western edge of the state, bound for the Keys. None of my steelhead or salmon fly gear was a match for tarpon and I knew it, but I had heard a lot about tarpon and their fighting abilities and wanted to give them a try. We would be using spin gear, live bait and we would be fishing in water too deep to wade, but that was all right.

The sky was still more gray than blue as the fiberglass boat moved out of the protected waters of the bay and into the Gulf of Mexico. Drew kept the throttle down and we passengers stood up as the boat bounced from wave to wave, the legs taking the pounding rather than the back. The first hour of light was the finest time in the day for a Pacific Northwest angler unaccustomed to the heat and humidity of a Florida June. At this hour the sun's rays were not to be feared either, and I wore nothing but a swimsuit. A few hours later I would slip into long pants, socks, long-sleeve shirt, place a broad-brimmed hat on my head and grease up any exposed skin with sunscreen. My thighs still smarted from a burn on the first day when I had on shorts and sat for awhile outside the shade of the small bimini. But for now it was nice to be ungreased and lightly clothed, the warm salt breeze comfortable against the skin. The wind was light and this was good as we wanted smooth water to spot tarpon, I was told as the boat planed across the gulf rollers. The tarpon would be migrating southbound in about fifteen feet of water which could be anywhere from a few hundred yards off the beach to a half mile or more depending on the slope of the bottom.

Drew cut the engine and we assumed lookout positions fore and aft, port and starboard. We were looking for a "show." To the uninitiated what we were looking at was simply a beautiful, blue-green sea, sparkling clear down to the sand-covered bottom, the surface smooth with small rolling swells, not deadpan flat but no chop to break the surface skin. It was all so gentle and warm compared to the ocean beaches in my part of the country with their thunderous surf, tides measured in feet instead of inches and water that even in the heat of summer is never warm. I was told to look for a show, a dorsal fin poking up through the water or splashes, signs that tarpon where about.

We were to look for "nervous" water, too. I had heard this term before and thought it a bit of a stretch, but nervous was the right word I realized as soon as we saw a school of at least a thousand small baitfish swimming by us near the surface. The baitfish themselves are always nervous, as their name suggests, for they exist as a potential meal for something higher on the food chain. A three-inch fish in a mountain creek is just a small fish as the water is not large enough to sustain many predators. The same sized fish in the ocean, full of many larger fish, is bait. But it is the agitated surface of the water that appears nervous, not the fish; the surface froth is more than a shimmer, less than a wind-blown chop. The froth is churned up by hundreds of tiny splashes from the little fish that give the water this anthropomorphic impression of being nervous. The fish move by quickly and the tennis-court-sized patch of nervous water soon fades into the distance.

Nervous water is good water because small fish attract larger fish and we are after larger fish, fish that could range from thirty pounds to one hundred and fifty pounds. The sun is rising higher and higher on a quiet morning, no engine noise, only seabird chatter from time to time. We're fishing but no one has yet touched a rod. We're fishing with our eyes, hunting for tarpon, searching the water close in and far off for splashes, fins, some sign, please. Minutes go by, bundles of minutes and soon an hour is gone. I spot a fin.

"There's one," I say. A minute passes while all eyes turn toward my outstretched arm.

"No, it's a dolphin," says John. Later they swim close by, dark sleek, and you can hear them breathing in the still air. On the other side of the boat a leopard ray slips by, ghostly silent, its elephant-eared body undulating in the water.

A show. Finally. Several eyes see it at once: dark fins attached to silver bodies cutting through the water, splashes on the smooth surface. The pod is maybe two hundred yards to the north, but moving our way. Drew fires up the big Johnson outboard engine and we maneuver to intercept them. He cuts the throttle and we glide into their intended line of travel. All is quiet pandemonium onboard as we rig up quickly to cast in the path of the cruising fish before they move beyond us.

"Get a crab," Drew says to Brian who reaches for a live blue crab. I help John capture a pinfish to bait the other rig. Drew and John cast out the bait, and then we all crouch down to minimize our silhouettes against the sky.

Railroad ties on the move. These huge fish swim toward us and all is a hush. Closer they come, milling about now, happy tarpon, unsuspecting tarpon. They look as though they could measure anywhere between three feet and five feet long, silver sides and darker tops. They're bearing down hard on us, these gigantic members of the herring family, *Megalops atlanticus*. Some of the dozen or more in the pod swim near the boat. Most of them are farther out. We watch the large bobbers on the two lines we have out in the water. The bobbers are in the right position as a number of the fish swim right underneath them. Others swim closer to the boat and I peek over the edge of the gunwale and see them swimming right under the hull: bright, lithe and monstrous. Everything is quiet, still. Talk is in whispers, bodies are hunkered down. The sun is warm, the water calm, we're on vacation in the land of palm-lined beaches, yet no one is relaxed, we're all wound tight. Tension blankets the boat like an invisible fog. The air seems thick, your limbs don't work properly, you feel your heart pounding in your chest.

The fish display no interest in this excitement on board or in the crab or pinfish that dangle in the water, attached to hooks and lines and to a boat full of would-be tarpon fighters. We recast for another chance.

"Blue crabs for sale," Drew says softly under his breath as he watches his line disappear into the water thirty feet out. No sale. The fish swim beyond our reach, and another boat some four hundred yards to the south begins to maneuver into position to repeat what we have done. But by now the tarpon are getting as nervous as the baitfish water was an hour ago; they're no longer happy tarpon, milling tarpon, daisy-chain tarpon. They're alarmed tarpon, spooked tarpon, tarpon swimming straight ahead at a very fast rate of speed, slicing through the water like a fleet of miniature cruisers at full speed, south bound in a hurry with no interest in slowing down to feed.

We spot a few more shows and cast to them in much the same manner. One fish slaps its tail hard on the surface when it passes by John's bait dangling below the large red and white bobber. It may have struck at the crab. John waits a moment and then sets the hook but the fish isn't there. It's difficult to set the hook in the tarpon's large, bony mouth, John says. You need to wait a moment until the line tightens. Even then getting a solid hookup can be difficult. For that reason Drew and John, the two locals who have had a little experience with tarpon, man the two rods. Brian and I, both tarpon neophytes, wait our turn to take over once the fish are hooked. I've got the rod butt holder strapped around my waist and my adrenal glands are pumping epinephrine, preparing me for battle. More tarpon pass by without taking our bait and my readiness begins to dissipate. I can feel the tightness dissolve. My concentration wanes; I'm no longer Zen focused on the suspense of the possible strike. The clock begins ticking again; time is back in play. I cannot hear my heart pounding as I could moments before. It's time for a cold can of beer from the ice chest, no matter that it's only mid-morning.

By noon the wind has kicked up and the boat traffic has increased, pleasure boats now in addition to fishermen, their wakes roughening the water. The surface of the gulf is no longer smooth and you'd have a tough time spotting a show in all the chop, so we head back to port. The next day repeats the first: a handful of shows, but not takes. Other tarpon hunters flank us up and down the beach and we see no hookups anywhere. After two days of chasing tarpon, coming close but not close enough, I must catch a plane for home. I know a tarpon on the line is the only antidote to the tarpon fever that I have contracted but it will have to wait until I return another day. For now, I'm left with thoughts of calm rolling water cut by dark dorsals, large scaled, yellow-hued silver-sided fish finning their way under the boat, whispered conversation on deck, frantic attempts to get a slippery, wiggly pinfish on the hook and get it out in front of a tarpon before it swims by, and the pre-strike tension that stretches a brief moment of time into a long memory.

Not only has this trip become a rich memory, but it illustrates the benefits of remaining open to new experiences when on a long-distance fishing adventure. Had I stuck fast to fishing with flies on the flats, none of this would have happened. The thrill of the tarpon hunt also demonstrates that there is a lot more to fishing than catching fish. We didn't catch any tarpon in two days of fishing for them. And with the experienced tarpon anglers doing the casting, I didn't even touch a rod for two days. I was the bait boy, the boat gopher. Yet if anyone asks about my sub-tropical fishing experience, I tell them I had the time of my life tarpon fishing. And I did: rod or no rod, catch or no catch. The well-traveled angler is open to new experiences because his travel lust springs from an adventuresome, curious nature. Curiosity about fish, new waters, new country, new people is part of the make-up of most anglers, even those who stay close to home.

For example, Walton appears to have done most of his angling close to home by walking from one country inn to the next. However, he was curious of the angling world outside England and that curiosity, and his wide reading, is reflected in his comments about various fish, their habitats, the countries they are found in and methods for catching them. He begins his chapter on trout with the observation that: "The trout is a fish highly valued both in this and foreign nations." He tells us about the habits and characteristics of trout native to England such as the Skegger-Trout and Fordidge Trout, as well as trout of the continent, such as the giant trout of Lake Geneva. One of Walton's continental authorities, Conrad Gesner, a sixteenth century German naturalist, claims these Lake Geneva trout grow to four and one-half feet long.

Walton also cites Gesner in the chapter on pike. Gesner mentions a pike taken in "Swedeland" in 1449 with a ring about its neck indicating it was tagged by Frederick the Second more than two hundred years earlier. Walton seems to enjoy tossing out such far-fetched comments and then walks away from them. After Gesner's observation on pike, the ever practical Walton says: "But of this no more, but that it is observed that the old or very great Pikes have in them more of state than goodness; the smaller or middle-sized Pikes being by the most and choicest palates observed to be the best meat."

Curiosity, adventure, the excitement of something new, all propel the traveling angler to look beyond his home waters from time to time. However, despite the travel industry's promotions, the well-traveled angler does not have to be a well-heeled angler. Some types of foreign angling may be difficult to do without getting locked into an expensive lodge and guide arrangement. It may be difficult to fly into Belize, find accommodations on your own, a boat to rent and good water to fish. But my Irish-blooded friend Michael has fished his ancestors' streams a number of times while on low-budget sightseeing trips spending little more than the cost of an Irish fishing license.

And it works the other way around. Once I encountered a group of three German anglers in central Oregon fishing the Deschutes River. They had rented a pickup camper in San Francisco and driven more than 600 miles to fish for summer-run steelhead on their own. They were having a wonderful time camping and fishing, and the angler I spoke with (he knew English quite well) was going to write up their experiences for a fishing journal published in Munich.

Within the U.S. and Canada, the traveling angler certainly does not have to be well heeled. Look at the lean-budgeted trout bums who fish some of the best waters coast to coast, season in and season out. At the other end of the spectrum, if you have plenty of money, you can purchase high-end trips at well-appointed lodges with attentive guides and fine meals. And if you stay at such a lodge and fish with a local guide who fishes the water week in and week out, you may outfish a lower-budgeted angler of comparable skill who has no guide but his wits.

But the angler with fewer financial resources does not have

to be in the dark when approaching new water. There are few fishing rivers in the country that do not have information about them in books, magazines or on various Internet sites. With the obligatory purchase of a little tackle, you can usually mine the hired help at local fishing shops for information, too. Another angling friend of mine, Rick, an entomologist by training, claims that one of the benefits to understanding aquatic insect life is that you can fish new waters more easily. He knows how to apply his knowledge of insect hatches and water conditions to most any river or lake. And he usually catches fish. Another tactic you can use if you have room in your modest budget for a bit of a splurge is to hire a local guide for a day. If you pay attention, you can learn a great deal during a day's fishing with someone who really knows the local water. And you can apply what you learn to your own unguided efforts for the rest of your trip.

Due to a tight budget and an independent nature, I have usually explored new waters on my own, sometimes assisted by a friend familiar with the local area. I've employed only a handful of guides over the years and stayed in fewer lodges. I enjoy poking around new areas, learning the different waters, milking the help at the local fly shops for information and experimenting. I don't mind camping, and if the weather is decent, I'd rather make a comfortable camp than stay in a lodge or motel. It is not a difficult matter to cook at camp, and for a break you usually are not far from a small town where you can take in a restaurant meal. Camping and fishing are closely intertwined for the mid-distance traveling angler. The best camps are those in quiet spots close to good fishing water. The mark of a well-selected camp is that you don't need to move the car for days on end.

A good camp is a deeply satisfying experience and part of the traveling angler; it is more than a home away from home, it provides a sense of freedom, too. The first hour at a new camp is busy with setting up the tent, arranging the cooking gear and gathering firewood. After that, you have it made. You don't have to go anywhere; you are outdoors, where you want to be. Just sit and listen to the water and watch the swallows dart about chasing insects. Open a cold bottle of beer and get out the potato chips. You have hours, maybe days in front of you to do whatever you want. There's no schedule to conform to: you eat when you're hungry, drink when you're thirsty, sleep when you're tired, arise when you're rested. You fish when you want, especially when the heat of the day dissipates and the shadows lengthen over the water. If you're energetic, you fish for hours and hours: morning, afternoon, evening—all day long. If you're lazy, you fish the last hour of twilight. You find it easy to spend hours sitting and listening to the river, talking to companions, staring into the campfire, puttering about with small camp chores.

When you have to leave, you work slowly folding up the tent, re-packing the grub box, stuffing sleeping bags, and in the same time it took you to set up camp you've disassembled it. The site looks as it did when you arrived and it's hard to remember that you had a temporary home there for several days. A good camp is like the cherry blossoms in spring: it is a transitory experience. You drive away from it and look back and there is nothing to see of your good camp. It has disappeared, as though you were never there at all. What you see of your good camp is in your mind's eye, in your memory. The thicket of small pines is where you shaded the ice chest. The drooping branch off the trunk of the stout ponderosa is where you hung the gas lantern to provide light for cooking a late dinner. The fire ring is cold and dirty now, but last night it was alive with bright flames and conversation under spangles of stars streaked across a dark sky.

While some traveling anglers stick to their camps and Colemans, others rent cabins, or motels or rooms at lodges. Anglers are a varied lot. Walton liked his country inns with sheets smelling of lavender. Today's trout bum travels the country from angling hotspot to angling hotspot in an old battered, paint-faded-on-the-hood Pontiac, bedroll stuffed in the back seat and empty granola boxes and six-packs in the trunk. The high-roller angler sinks into the deeply cushioned leather seat of his new Range Rover on the way to the lodge for cocktails, a Caesar salad, filet mignon dinner and clean, crisp sheets on the Simmons Beautyrest in his private room. Each in his own way, traveling anglers all have their own style, but what's important is that they're exploring new water, satisfying that wanderlust that afflicts even the most dedicated home-water angler from time to time. Memories of the new waters and new fish and new people and new country will fuel your imagination for years. And while you are remembering past trips, you likely will be busy planning new ones, studying maps and books for new rivers to explore, new fish to catch and new country to see. Like most aspects of the angling life, you will never run out of possibilities; you'll only run out of time.

# III. The Homewater Angler

THERE IS NO WATER LIKE HOME WATER. ALL ANGLERS SHOULD have a home water, a place they are intimate with, a place they have fished season in and season out, year in and year out, decade after decade. A home water anchors the dedicated angler, allows him to really know a river or lake or stream or bay. It will provide him with fish on the hook because he will get to know the best spots, the best times, the little secrets that are slowly revealed and jealously guarded. And over the years, it will provide him with more than fish, too.

Home water usually is a place near enough to your home so that you can fish it often. It is difficult to call a stream your home water if you only fish it once every few years. You've got to be there on a regular basis. It could be a small lake outside town that you fish after work on long summer evenings. It could be a stream in the mountains that frame the valley where you live. It could also be a river thousands of miles away located near your summer home that you travel to every year. Wherever it is, whatever it is, it has to be fished many times over many years to become home water. Just as the boy in *The Velveteen Rabbit* makes a stuffed bunny real by loving it over a long time, so you make a certain river or lake your home water by fishing it, caring for it, thinking about it over many years.

Home water is a place that is near home and it is a place that becomes home. The dictionary tells us that home is the place where you live or the place where you were reared. And it also defines home as "a place thought of as home...a place where one likes to be." After a few years you begin to sense the home feeling when you arrive at your home water. You don't feel as though you have gone away to go fishing; you feel as though you have come home. You feel that the weeks or months that have passed since your last visit have been spent in the pursuit of more pedestrian tasks and that now you have returned to bedrock. You're centered on your home water. In your other life you make money, spend money, get sick, get well, move from one house to another, change cars, change jobs and watch your children grow, but when you pull up to your favorite camp spot on your home water all is as it was before. Water flows between the shaded alder banks in a hurry to get to the ocean. Fish rise in the back eddies, cruising the foam line for spent mayflies whose translucent veined wings protrude at right angles to their slim bodies, their movement now dictated by the current swirls, a world away from yesterday when they moved through the air under their own propulsion, their wings beating so swiftly they appeared not to beat at all but to glide effortlessly, their twin tails trailing behind, rudders in the warm summer air. Dead caddis, hollow stonefly shucks and midge clusters also crowd the cream-colored froth where converging currents collect the aquatic life suspended in the river flow.

Having a home water bonds you to the land. You become part of the equation of water, trees, fish, birds and other life that call the river home. To travel from exotic fishing spot to spot is exciting, but many anglers crave a closeness with one particular place. Just as the wandering youth eventually settles down to live his life in one particular town, in one particular neighborhood, so the wandering angler often adopts a stream, river or lake as his own. Anglers differ, of course, and while some feel a need to settle on a home water, others hopscotch about fishing a number of waters and not settling on any one river or lake. There is something to be said for the freedom of the nomadic angler, but also something to be said for getting to know one particular water well. The world of nature mirrors this human condition, too. Many fish and animals live in a very small world and know every inch of their habitat well. Most trout don't move far from the gravel they emerge from as alevin. Biologists say that many blacktail deer live out their lives in an area less than one square mile. By contrast, some birds migrate thousands of miles every year. Salmon and steelhead reared in western mountain streams spend most of their adult lives on the high seas, schooling along the northern Asiatic shores, feeding in the Bering Sea. But even among the migratory species, the homing instinct is strong. Waterfowl migrate along predictable flyways. Salmon seek the same natal water where they reared.

The homing instinct is strong among us and we flout it at some risk. Today we are a country of chain stores, chain restaurants, chain motels and a nationally unified television culture. Superficially at least, you feel at home whether you get off the plane in Charleston or Denver. With airline travel we tend to travel far and wide, nibbling at many landscapes. While international travel was once the pleasure of the rich, it now is available

to many of us. To have traveled broadly usually improves character, but it can also distract you from knowing the country in
front of your nose. Those who live close to the land usually
know it best. When you settle on a home water you get to
know it better than you will any other piece of the outdoors,
except maybe your backyard. You know it boulder by boulder,
eddy by eddy, riffle by riffle. There is a great satisfaction over
the years of returning to the same river and knowing what is
around the next bend. Over time you begin to feel a sense of
belonging. As you get to know a piece of water well over many
years you feel a part of it. You feel as though you are of it, like
the fish and otters and swallows and stoneflies. You may not be
there every day, but you aren't a stranger either. This is your
place in the natural world, it is your home range, your habitat.
We should not think that our street address is our only home.
Home is where things are familiar, where you belong. Even if
your home water is located in a remote, wild area, it can
become home and you will cease being apprehensive about its
isolation. I have weathered thunderstorms, wildfires, snow,
heat, floods, skunks, rattlesnakes, earwigs and sickness on my
home water and I don't feel apprehensive at all when pitching
camp there now even though camp is miles from the nearest
town. With familiarity you can tame a wild place so that you
feel at home there. Fear of the wild is an odd notion that most
of us have: an owl hoot or coyote howl can cause many to lay
awake in their sleeping bags far into the night. Once you know
a place, it is not truly wild anymore. A western Indian reportedly once took exception to the white's notion of the great
wilderness west of the Mississippi. To him, the country in question was not a wilderness, it was home.

As you get to know a home water and feel a growing sense
of familiarity with it you want to learn more about it and
explore it. If your home water is a river this can be quite a task.

But if you like rivers, as most anglers do, you naturally want to
know the river's source, its mid-reaches, its terminus. In my
part of the country most rivers begin high in the mountains as
the winter's snow slowly melts forming tiny rivulets through
alpine meadows. The rivulets braid, converge, empty into one
another to form creeks which in turn do the same as the water
rushes down the mountainsides forming streams and eventually
rivers. In some places these streams collect in a lake still high in
the mountains and from this lake may spring your river. The
river may flow into yet another lake where once again the
waters are slowed and stilled before gravity pulls them into yet
another outfall. On and on your river flows. In the West especially, the landscape surrounding rivers changes markedly as
they flow downhill from steep mountain forests with fir and
pine alongside the river banks to sagebrush and scraggly juniper
only a little farther downstream. In its middle reaches your river
may do all sorts of things: it may cut through a deep canyon
providing you with a cross-section of past geologic ages. It may
enter a flat area and lose its way, fanning out into a marsh, soak-
ing into the earth. If the slope of the land is steep it may continue tumbling, cascading along, white with froth, loud with
the chatter of water against rocks. Most rivers slow down in
their middle and later stretches, their character matching the
gradient of the terrain. Long before most rivers flow into the
salt they have spent their river's energy that comes from the
slope of the land. Down on the flats the current moves slowly,
influenced by the tides. On large rivers, such as the Columbia
near my hometown, the distant tides of the ocean are felt many
miles inland in places where there is no tang of salt in the air,
no sound of breakers. Likewise, the freshwater plume of large
rivers like the Columbia extends miles out into the salt water,
mixing the melted snow water of the inland mountains with the
ancient water of the ocean.

Not only does your home river change as you trace its flow toward the sea, but its features change little by little, year after year. You know that you're settled into a home water when you begin noticing these changes. At first glance, a certain stretch of river looks much the same from one year to the next. But if you go there long enough you notice changes. Sometimes these changes are subtle, such as a grove of streamside alders that appear a little taller and broader every year. Or you notice a cut-bank eroding a little more every year. But other times the changes are sudden, usually caused by cataclysmic events such as floods. Not long ago a flood on my home water created an entire new set of rapids overnight. A wheat rancher who lives near the river told me it was one of those rare midsummer hail and rainstorms. Within minutes of the cloudburst the storm filled the dry, rocky canyon creeks with muddy runoff. Along one bank of the river runs a railroad and the flow from these creeks is channeled under the roadbed through large culverts. At one spot the flow of several creeks draining the surrounding feeder canyons is channeled through twin culverts, each big enough to drive a car through. While normally only a trickle of water flows through these culverts in the summer, the storm sent such a large volume of water down the steep hillsides that the culverts compressed the flow like twin water cannons, shooting water, rocks and boulders out into the river. The next morning, when all was back to normal, and the sky was once again a bright cloudless blue, the boulders remained lodged in the riverbed, forming a new whitewater rapid that likely will be there for many decades, if not centuries.

You get to know your home water physically—its rapids, islands, gravel bars, eddies and pools—and over time it sinks into your psyche and you know it in other ways, as well. Your presence there with various companions and at different times in your life invests the rocks and water and trees and grasses with so many memories that familiar spots seem alive with another dimension that you never experience on new water. When you are on a new piece of water you see the river as a river, but your home water is a river of memory. You could say that the house where you have lived for decades is full of memories, too, and your old college campus is full of memories and so is your hometown. But there is something distinctive about the memories contained in natural settings without any signs of human habitation.

At the end of Norman Maclean's novella, *A River Runs Through It*, the narrator says that he is haunted by waters. "Under the rocks are the words, and some of the words are theirs" he says of those he loved and whom are now dead.

I don't feel haunted yet by my home water, but I do feel overwhelmed at times by the ability of this memory-filled, inanimate landscape of water and rock to affect me. Like most anglers, I have changed home waters during my lifetime and always wonder what it would be like to have had the same home water at eighty as eight. For those who never strayed far from their birthplace, such a life-long home water must be thick with memories. I am only into my third decade with my current home water. While it is nearly devoid of human habitation, save a few ranch buildings, it is well peopled for me. On a recent trip with my friend Chris we floated down the river in my drift boat.

"Isn't that where your brother hooked a nice fish?" Chris says of a gravel bar on the upstream edge of a small island close to the east bank.

"Sure is," I answer. My brother did hook a good fish there more than a decade ago on a trip with Chris and me. And years before that trip at the same spot my first child, now an adult but then a baby, sat on the bank with his mother while I hooked a good fish. The island looks much the same now as it did back then, but we do not.

Farther downriver we put in at a long riffle on the west side and Chris goes to fish the upper end with a small mayfly. I work a stonefly nymph through the lower end where the riffle gives way to deeper holding water—where the kitchen meets the dining room, as one friend says of such spots. I heave the weighted stonefly upstream and hold the rod high as the fly bounces along near the bottom, watching the little white plastic corkie that I'm using as a strike indicator. I've got a small green bead head on the trailer and I work the water the best I can. The morning sun covers the river in most places, a few shaded areas still linger on the east bank that is shadowed by the steep canyon walls. I remember my pre-teen daughter a few years earlier as she and a friend played in this same water where I am now standing, their life jackets on, laughing, bobbing about in the rocky current. We co-exist, this memory and I, while I continue the casting, mending and waiting for the corkie to disappear under the surface in the sharp take of a large trout.

You don't have this experience on new water. While alive in its own way, a new river is not full of the past, infused with memory, each trip overlaid with the memories of the last. River memory enriches your homewater experience like the shadows on the rocky slopes enrich the landscape, giving it a depth and complexity absent in the harsh, featureless light of high noon.

After floating through a few more bends in the river, Chris and I notice that the dead stick camp is occupied with two tents, and I think of all the fine camps I've had at that spot and feel annoyed that someone else is in "my camp." Of course, it is not my camp. The anglers who have pitched their tents are only there for a few days just as I have camped there over the years for a day or two at a time. For most of us home water does not imply ownership. You don't have to own a piece of water to know it. In the natural world ownership is a shallow notion anyway. How do you own a river? You can own title to the land bordering the river and restrict access to others and thereby say that you own the river. But do you own it in the way you own a car or boat or house? How can you own the snow melt moving to the sea? How do you own the fish and the caddis larvae and the osprey that all are part of the river? And even if you do convince yourself that you own the river, that doesn't mean that you know it. In fact, the man who truly believes that he owns a river probably lacks the capacity to know the river. To know a piece of water has nothing to do with ownership. You learn to know a river when you fish it, swim it, boat it, and walk down to its banks to fill your water bucket with rinse water for the camp dishes. You scramble along its brush-infested banks and wade its broad gravel bars where the flow sweeps by you on its way to the sea.

Hopefully you are able to visit your river regardless of the season and you know it month by month. The summer riverbank trail where you kicked up dust in the hot August evenings is frozen hard in December. The dust no longer lays on top of the soil ready to swirl in the wind gusts; the cold has bonded the dust with the frozen ground and it feels hard to the step. Your broad-brimmed hat is replaced with a wool stocking cap and your thin cotton shirt is replaced with a down vest tightly zipped up to your neck to break the cold wind. On each visit you tighten the knot between you and your river. In between your visits other anglers also fish the river and some of them get to know it well too, some even better than you. A river's assimilative capacity is great and many anglers can know the same water as long as they care for it, conserve its fish, protect it and keep it clean.

You know all this, but still you feel a tinge of proprietorship and jealously when another party is lodged at "your" camp, or fishing "your" water. And at the dead stick camp the party appears to be a large one with two boats and at least two tents.

One of the anglers in the group rows one of the boats across the river as we approach. He puts in at one of the best back eddies on the river, one that we were going to fish.

"Let's forget it," I say to Chris.

"Okay," Chris says and we drift by. I look back at the strange angler beginning to cast into the eddy, wondering if he will hook any fish. Selfishly, I hope he doesn't. Oh, I'm sure if we were all sitting around the camp together drinking beer, eating tortilla chips and salsa and talking fish he would be a great guy and we would probably even discover a few mutual friends who fish our common water. But for now he's a rival angler and he's in "my" water. It is always surprising how quickly the transcendentalism of angling erodes into orneriness.

We float around two more bends in the river and come to Big Indian Riffle. No one is fishing the water but my memory instantly overpopulates it with what seem like short, intensive film clips playing inside my head of other days on Big Indian. The riffle is in front of me now, stretching out more than half way across the channel allowing you to wade from ankle deep water up to your thighs if you can withstand the force of the current. Big Indian is imprinted with the image of my father gingerly wading out into its flow, him a small-mountain-stream angler unaccustomed to a trout river so wide that you can't wade across it. And I see two of my fishing companions, both named Bill, on the water, one who introduced me to this river decades ago planted butt deep in the fast water, lost in the concentration of working a soft hackle through the evening chop. Tall, thick, the kind of guy who darkens a doorway, Bill is able to maintain position in the strong current that would sweep away lesser waders. He casts again and again with little apparent effort, conserving his strength, keeping the pattern in the water and not in the air. And the other Bill is there too, pushing aggressively upstream through the current working a dry pattern to rising fish in the slack water just above the upstream lip of the riffle. Rain is falling through the dry desert air, drilling the flat water with drops from the sky, mixing the water of the air with that of the land. Bill has on a poncho that flaps about like a wind-rustled miniature tent as his arms and shoulders move underneath to cast the fly out again and again.

And I see the sixteen-inch fish I hooked once on the inside edge of the riffle in water so shallow you wouldn't think a sculpin could be there. A good portion of the trout's back was out of the water and it slithered like a finned reptile toward the safety of deeper water after it felt the sting of the steel hook. But the riffle is a broad one and it took the fish a while to gain deeper water, especially with me pressuring it on the other end of the fly line. When I landed and measured the fish it was in water still not above the tops of my wading boots. Since then whenever I hear about thin-water trout I think of that fish in this spot and remind myself not to rush through the shallow water, but to put a few casts through it first.

"Let's go on. It's not good salmonfly water," I say to Chris as we float by Big Indian. The riffle shines later in the season when the caddis hatches start coming off and the fish chase rising pupae in the broken water. We put in below it and fish a rim of tall grass along a flat, slow drift. The water is wadeable only two or three feet out from the bank, so you're in tight against the long grass. Unlike Africa, you don't have to fear lions in this tall grass, but you do feel large salmonflies and golden stoneflies crawling on your hat, neck and shoulders. One tries to crawl between my eyebrow and my glasses and I swat it away. I pick another one of these dark red and gray stoneflies off my neck and toss it in the water. It flutters in the film, a very animate meal for a fish, but it doesn't attract any takers. We hook some fish here beside the tall grass, and some we don't. I miss a good many strikes it seems, but then again maybe they aren't really hitting the fly with an open mouth but are playing with it, nosing it about to see what it is. One fish rises twice in a row to brush the fly, but not open mouthed enough for me to set the hook.

The water is less turbulent here and it reminds me of what I imagine many of the English trout streams might resemble, such as the Dove River in Derbyshire, the home water of Charles Cotton, Walton's fly-fishing collaborator. On the banks of the Dove is the much-celebrated Fishing-house used by these two seventeenth-century angling writers. This small stone building—part shelter, part temple—speaks deeply to many anglers, most whom have seen it only through pictures. Constructed of stone and marble, it has a permanence and architecture to it sorely lacking in the fishing shacks of the past few centuries. And it has the perfect inscription over the door: Piscatoribus Sacrum. Loosely translated I'm told the phrase means a place sacred to fishermen, but this is one of those cases where the original speaks more directly to us than does the translation so Piscatoribus Sacrum it remains.

Chris and I are pioneers, cowboys, wilderness explorers by Walton's standards of stone fishing houses and country inns. Our shelter is only a small nylon tent and it is in the boat now while we fish and move downriver. There is a history to our home water, too, just as there is to the Walton's English rivers with their longer record of human occupation. And if you have a home water, you want to learn its history for that enlivens it, invests it with substance. Here in north central Oregon the earliest signs of human contact with the river come in the form of petroglyphs left hundreds, perhaps thousands of years ago by the earliest Americans. Recorded history begins with the Lewis and Clark expedition that passed the mouth of the Deschutes on its way down the Columbia River in October of 1805. They recorded little about the river in their journals for they were occupied with getting their canoes around the thundering Celilo Falls on the Columbia, just downstream from the confluence with the Deschutes.

Unlike many rivers, the deeply canyoned Deschutes was an impediment to early travel rather than a route for travel. In December of 1825 Peter Skene Ogden with the Hudson's Bay Company traveled up the river's west bank from the mouth, though his route appears to have been several miles back from the river, out of the canyon and up on the sagebrush flats. He crossed the river at the same spot my brother caught his good fish, and his party reportedly lost four horses in the tough winter crossing. Like many early explorers, Ogden left little historical record of his observations about the river. He was in search of beaver and the Deschutes appears to have been little more than an obstacle on the way to better beaver country to the east.

Thinly populated in its lower 100 miles, the riverbanks reveal the struggle of early settlement. Like the trappers and miners before them, the pioneers were not interested in anything as ethereal as trout or fly fishing. They were intent on coaxing a living from this rough, rocky, dry country. Their abandoned homesteads dot the uplands and now and again can be seen from the river. Houses, barns and sheds with weathered gray wood boards sandblasted by decades of wind still stand because of the dry climate. They look lonely in this big open country. They have stories to tell but are mute, unable to communicate to us about the lives of those who once lived there. You look around in these abandoned homesteads, look past the bird droppings on the dirty floorboards and imagine what it would have been like to have lived here in the old days when the county was newly settled. You imagine that life for many of these settlers was built on a promise that slowly eroded into disappointment under the unrelenting elements.

Along one bank of the river you walk on an abandoned railroad grade, a monument to one of the country's last great railroad wars fought between subsidiaries of the great Northern Railroad and the Union Pacific from 1909 to 1911. You think of the hundreds of sweat-drenched men working with shovels, picks and blasting powder to make grade, bore tunnel and lay track. And on a few sections of the river you see modern-day Fishing-houses. Most are simple wood frame structures and a few are made of cinder block. None are made of stone and marble. One Fishing-house that I had the good fortune to visit once, a simple small wooden frame building located a short cast from some fine holding water, has since been washed away by a flood.

When a water becomes your home water you want to know its history, just as you want to know its fish life, insect hatches, wildlife, plants, geology, tributaries, springs, uplands and weather. All waters have histories: the personal history you bring to them with your visits, and the history of others who have known the water, some who knew it hundreds of years ago.

Chris and I move downriver again and float around the east channel of the big island. We thread the white water between the large boulder on the left that sticks out of the river five feet high or so and the large submerged boulder some ten feet to the right. Afterwards comes the standing waves at the island's tip, nothing much compared to the tumultuous water farther downriver, but enough to put up a small spray. On the east bank below the island is where we once fished some years back with my son who was then nearing the end of grade school. It was a hot July trip and we spent much of mid-day in the shade, under the streamside alder trees that provide a shelter and coolness in this blistering hot summer canyon where temperatures stretch into the triple digits. These alders like their feet wet and in places along the bank their knarled exposed roots reach out into the river and soak up its moisture. The bushy canopy overhead absorbs the intense midday sunlight. You duck under the low hanging branches and settle in under an alder, next to the stream to escape the afternoon heat. Pull up a folding camp chair and plant it next to the water so that like the alder you can soak your feet in the stream while you sit in the shade. Dip your bandana in the water and wrap it around your head. Splash water on your neck and wrists. Splash it on your face. Relax in the chair, under the alder whose branches droop nearly to the ground like an old weeping willow tree. You are encased in the tree's shade next to the coolness of flowing water and you can comfortably survive the glare of the sun that is heating the basalt on the uplands to furnace temperatures. The volcanic rock, molten once itself milleniums ago, grows hotter and hotter with the summer sun. The columnar basalt, brick bat basalt, talus basalt and ragged basalt castellations soak up the heat of the summer sun, store it in their dense fabric and radiate it back slowly just as a stone fireplace stays warm long after the fire has died.

The river provides a ribbon of life through this harsh, hard county; once you're fifty feet back from the shoreline you won't find any alder at all. Your only hope for shade is the occasional juniper, its aroma mingling with the smell of sage. Pick a few berries, split them open and smell the scent. Mixed with the sage and the dry, rarified air, the juniper aroma is satisfying, comforting, and western. You can be away from this country for a long time and you may forget many of its features, but you will never forget its smell. Every home water has a smell that you become acquainted with over time, a scent that imprints itself deep into your olfactory memory. It is not something you think much about, but it makes a strong impression. Compared to animals, our sense of smell is virtually undeveloped, yet our scent memory is strong and the smell of your home water will stay with you for decades.

Your home water also has a distinctive sound to it that becomes part of you over time just as you remember its smells and sights and the feel of its slippery, firm-fleshed fish. The best way to hear your river is to sleep next to it under the stars and moon. The rushing sound of water flowing over rocks always seems louder at night when you are in your sleeping bag, staring into the black of the wilderness night, searching for a shooting star, having to settle for the mechanical blinking of an orbiting satellite. Sometimes you expect the river to become quieter at night, as the birds find their roosts and cease their singing when the sun sets. But the river doesn't quiet. It seems to grow louder because everything else is quieter and because noises are always louder in the dark. All through the night it makes its river noises, lapping at the coarse sandy beach, thundering around a mid-stream boulder, tripping over the fist-sized rocks of the broad gravel bar. When you awake in the morning to the cool dawn air, the river sounds the same as it did when you drifted off to sleep. And it will sound much the same the next time you return.

And then there is the music of the birds that live along the banks of your home water, too. On my home water the song of the western meadowlark defines the country along with the shrill cries of magpies and the chuck, chuck, chucking of the chukar partridge. You realize after awhile, after you've done some exploring away from the crowds, that most of the sounds of fishing come from moving water and from birds. At times you may hear a coyote howling or squirrels chattering. But most of the time it is quiet on the angling waters except for the birds and the slap of running water on river rock.

We are now within a mile or so of the campground and boat ramp where our trip will end. Both sides of the river are thick with memories from past trips to this campground where we often paddled a canoe or raft to the other side to fish. Here my history merges with settlement history for behind the campground, up the tributary draw, the last hostile Indian in the area, a renegade named Chief Paulina of the Walapi tribe, was ambushed and shot in 1867. Here too, the railroad climbs out of the canyon along the banks of the same tributary to the south and east.

Here I witnessed a large wildfire one summer while at the campground. Who knows how it started, but by the late afternoon hundreds of acres of cheat grass was burning, the fire moving up the slope. The fire burned low to the ground and failed to ignite some of the junipers, but others lit up like torches. Smoke drifted thick and lazy in the hot air. We fished on the other side of the river, near the canoe that we had paddled across, and we watched the fire climb up the canyon. A helicopter with a large bucket suspended below it hovered over the river. It dipped the bucket into the river filling it with water. Then the helicopter flew to the edge of the fire and dumped the water on the flames and returned to the river for more water. When it filled its bucket in the river the rotor blades sucked the river water into a fine windy spray and you had to hold onto your hat. It was noisy and unsettling to share your riffle water with a firefighting helicopter, but the fire had to be fought. The fire burned into the night in places, finally extinguishing itself when it consumed all the dry grass on the upper canyon slopes and met the rimrock. While alive with fire millions of years ago when molten lava flowed in sheets across the Columbia plateau, the solid basalt columns at the rim now serve as a fire-break, keeping the fire from spreading to the irrigated farmland beyond. In the morning, ash covered our sleeping bags and the air still had an acrid smell to it. The landscape was patched with large, black, smoldering burns.

You get to know a home water in all its shadings: blackened by wildfire, dazzling white with fresh fallen snow, yellow with summer heat, green with the freshness of spring, gray with rain, and red and gold in the fall. You get to know its sounds, its smells and the feel of its damp, fine rounded gravel between your toes. It is early summer now as Chris and I pull into the take-out. There is still a little green in the creases of the sidehills where the slopes converge into one another, where springs seep out of the rock and sprout tangles of wild roses and tall grass. Chris and I load the boat onto the trailer, transfer gear to the van and head out of the canyon. We head up the tributary stream where Chief Paulina was shot. We snake out of the canyon on a steep dirt road, cross under a steel railroad trestle and then through a single lane tunnel. In the rear view mirror I watch the river disappear from view, but it will remain clear in my mind's eye for days to come. Through memory and imagination you can take your home water home. You can, with some practice, conjure up its smells and sights. You can feel the pull of a good fish racing downstream, running line off the spool as it enters the big water, as it cleans your clock. Once you have made a water yours through familiarity and affection it becomes your movable feast. It sustains and buoys you when you can't be there, when you are taking out the garbage or off to a meeting or standing in line at the bank. It is there with its water flowing relentlessly downstream, trout chasing mayfly duns as they awkwardly emerge from their nymphal shucks in the film, sunlight filtering through the thick alder branches, water rustling over smooth rocks that are wedged one against the other in the current. It is there in your head and it is there on the ground, and you know that when you return that it will be as it was before.

# IV. THE WELL-DRESSED ANGLER

REGARDLESS OF WHETHER YOU FISH CLOSE TO HOME OR far off you will have to contend with a number of practical matters that accompany any fishing trip, matters that are not directly related to getting your line in the water. Among these attendant matters are the right clothing, food and drink for these are all essential to the success of any fishing trip. How we take care of such elemental concerns is part of the pleasures of the angling life, for even the reflective angler lives in the physical world as well as the metaphysical. Moreover, anglers are in the end a methodical bunch; they would rather take care of practical matters first. The stories, the lies, the endless ruminations come later, at the end of the trip. The beginning of a fishing trip is filled with planning and preparations concerning tackle, food, tides, hatches, river levels, weather and all types of gear. The first step in all this preparation is what to wear.

Practical minded anglers like to imagine that they select their fishing clothes, waders and boots from an entirely functional point of view and reserve the remainder of their energy for reading the water, identifying insects, matching the hatch, making the proper presentation and so on. Other anglers, often new to fly fishing, pay undue attention to their dress, attracted in part to the sport by its apparel that today has a certain off-stream status too with the stylish waxed cotton English coats and cocky wide-brimmed hats. Especially if he is going to an upscale fishing lodge, the stylish angler wants to look the part even if his fishing skills may be minimal.

Practical or stylish, what you wear on the river reflects your angling persona. This is true even for the angler who pays little attention to what he wears. That alone says something about him—that he could care less what others think, that he's a purely practical guy. He wants his boots and waders and vest to work well in a variety harsh conditions, fit comfortably and that is that. But even the most no-nonsense angler will admit a vain look in the mirror when trying on a new fishing hat, that most expressive part of the angler's wardrobe. Besides, part of the joy of fishing is gear, and your gear is not only the tackle you use but what you wear as well. Just as you enjoy using a finely crafted rod, you also should take pleasure in your waders, vest and hat because, afterall, catching fish is only one of the pleasures of the fishing life.

The construction of the well-dressed angler begins with solid footing, especially important in an avocation where the path to success takes you over slippery rocks covered much of the time by a Teflon-like slime. When you first started fishing in your youth, wading shoes were nothing more than old tennis shoes, simple and economical but disastrous in the water. You see young anglers still wearing tennis shoes today when wading, but rarely older anglers. A few slips, bruised bones and cold dunkings usually take care of that. I don't consider myself a clumsy person, but in some waters—those rivers where large, uneven, slippery rocks are washed by a swift cold current—it is difficult to take two steps in a row without faltering, even with a wading staff. Usually I am a good wader, aggressive but not foolhardy. But I have found that the most dangerous part of wading often is when you get close to shore and you are done wading the most difficult water. Then your concentration wanes and trouble strikes. It is as if the river is waiting for you to relax and then it twists your ankle and down you go.

I recall one time on the Deschutes and we had taken a canoe to the far side to fish the evening rise. We split up and agreed to meet several hours later at sunset back at the canoe.

"Good luck," I said to my companions as they walked off upriver.

"You too," said Bill as they disappeared down the dry dirt trail.

I went downstream from the canoe and soon I was wading in the river. I waded down a long gravel bar, fishing out into the current and in toward the alders, too. Eventually the gravel bar ran out, the run deepened and it was time to wade back to shore. The wading wasn't difficult, but right next to shore the current picked up a bit. I was not paying close attention to my footing as the current still was not too fast, nor was the water too deep.

Kerplunk!

Suddenly I was spread eagle, face down in the river. I was barely conscious of falling. One minute I was standing and the next minute I was in the drink. The water was less than two feet deep and yet I was wet up to my eyebrows. If you were trying to dunk yourself in this shallow water it would be difficult to do, but apparently it was not difficult to do by accident. Somehow I had lost my footing and the wading staff had not been able to stabilize my wobbling form. I was down but not for long. I quickly rose, retrieved my hat and then took three steps to the bank. I couldn't believe I had fallen in such shallow water so close to shore and gotten so wet. At least a good fall should be taken while attempting to wade the big, difficult steelhead water out near the edge of the main current. Maybe you could even brag about such a fall later. You could say that you were pushing the limit, testing just how far an angler could wade in that particular run. But here? A no-name little riffle without obvious wading dangers? It was humiliating.

My safety belt was secure around my waist so not too much water had seeped inside the waders. But my long-sleeved fishing shirt and T-shirt were soaked. I had three hours before dark and I knew my partners would not want to return to camp during the best fishing time of the day unless they saw my lips turning blue. It wasn't going to get that bad as is was not cold out, but the temperature was going to cool off quickly when the sun dropped behind the canyon's rim. I walked up the bank onto a sagebrush flat and took off my shirt and T-shirt and spread them out on the sage limbs to dry in the light breeze. I took off my waders and turned them inside out so the water that had seeped in them would dry. Instead of fishing for the next hour I huddled in the sage and watched my clothes and waders dry. It was very exciting. I got chilled eventually and had to put the clothes on before they completely dried out. I fished out the remainder of the evening in a damp shirt as the temperature continued to drop. I survived just fine, but it was not the evening's fishing I had looked forward too for I was too distracted by the cold to enjoy the angling. At last my companions returned and I was glad to see them. We paddled across the river in the darkening air back to camp where dry clothes were waiting.

You have a few encounters such as these and you don't scrimp on wading boots. You get the best you can find. They are an absolute priority in the angler's wardrobe. For most wading, the felt-soled wading boot is standard today, augmented by metal studs and for the most treacherous waters, strap-on rubber sandals with steel cleats. There's little style consideration in boots: they are usually brown in color and constructed of various synthetic materials and leather. Getting the proper fit can be difficult, especially if you want to use the same pair of boots with heavy neoprene waders and without any waders at all for wet-wading in the summer. Fit is difficult too because a boot that slips on comfortably when dry, as you would try it on in a store, will likely be too large in the water. Conversely, a pair of wading boots that fit well when wet will likely be too tight to put on dry. The pair of wading boots I now own fit well when wet, but I need to dunk them in the water before I can put them on. Otherwise I feel like one of the ugly sisters in *Cinderella* struggling to wedge a size-eight foot into a size-five glass slipper.

While excellent for traction and ankle support, most of the wading boots that I have tried share the common trait of becoming awfully waterlogged and heavy by the end of the day. On my wish list for the perfect fishing outfit would be a pair of sturdy, river-bottom-grabbing boots that are lightweight and do not retain water. One way I have learned to lighten the load a bit is using a neoprene wading outer sock rather than the traditional wool outer sock that absorbs a great deal of water and weight.

Just up from the boots is a marvelous invention called gravel guards. These neoprene cuffs perform the critical task of keeping fine river gravel out of your boots where it can rub holes in your stocking-foot waders. In addition, the gravel guards keep your boot laces tucked neatly and safely away. I was reminded of this feature the other day when one of my gravel guards came loose and the long loop on one lace caught an underwater wood tangle, tripping me into the shallow water.

The well-outfitted angler spends much of his personal outfitting attention on his waders. Sometimes it seems I've spent half my fishing life struggling in and out of waders. It is not that I dislike them, it is just that they are a necessary nuisance for those of us in colder climates. When possible, I prefer to wade wet, unencumbered by an impermeable membrane between my skin and the water. Then, in the summer, I wear a pair of quick-drying, non-cotton, long pants to protect my legs against streamside thorns and poison oak. Southern anglers are fortunate for they can forget about waders entirely. On a fishing trip to Florida not long ago I was delighted day after day that I did not have to fool around with waders or wading boots: just slip on a pair of swim trunks and water socks and you were ready to jump into the warm water and shuffle along on the sand-covered bottom of the bay.

But when water temperature dictates waders, waders it is. Nowadays we have a choice of much better waders than a few decades ago, especially with the breathable waders at the upper end of the price range. Eventually, most of us will be wearing these models after our current neoprene sauna suits wear out. Neoprene waders are a joy in cold weather, but if it gets warm in mid-day the condensation inside the waders can become unbearable. Their form-fitting style helps you wade with more agility, another improvement over yesterday's waders that were baggy and had little elasticity. You feel sleek when wading the big waters, able to stretch around boulders and scramble up and down the bank more easily. All this is a long way from some of the boot-foot rubber waders of years ago that had little flexibility. I remember one bargain-priced pair of boot-foots I purchased years ago. The first day on the river I bent over and the crotch ripped out. The remainder of the day was spent in water that was knee-deep or less.

The form-fitting quality of waders do strange things to anglers' physiques. Generally, they make the angler appear more leggy, slimmer, taller, like one gloved unit. Up close, however, the neoprene sleekness often gives way to a certain rotundness for the more portly anglers as the form-fitting fabric clings to the contours of the middle-age potbelly. If you are among these anglers, you know what I mean.

Next is the fishing vest. A well-made fishing vest worn in all months of the year, and in climates as diverse as Alaska to Florida, can provide much pleasure, and after years of service it houses many memories, too. It is your home away from home containing not only your angling gear but food, water, sun-screen, insect repellent, emergency gear, matches, sunglasses, and rain jacket. It is the angler's security blanket. Slip into the well-provisioned vest and you are ready for a day of angling in whatever conditions the hatches and weather may dictate.

I've tried fishing without a vest, to go lighter and simpler, but I always feel wanting. I don't always carry a great number of fly boxes in my vest; sometimes such as in summer steelhead-ing I carry only a single fly box. But it is the other things that you may need as soon as you leave the vest in the boat or at camp and venture out vestless that can be bothersome: clippers, hook remover, hook sharpener, insect repellent, strike indica-tors, split shot or a Band-Aid for the unforeseen cut that won't stop bleeding.

In my present stage of angling evolution I am striving to perfect the lightly provisioned vest, for the vest is the most obvious manifestation of how obsessed you are by gear—an occupational hazard of anglers. The truly lightly provisioned vest is the vest of youth for when you first start fishing you have not had enough time or money to accumulate much gear. That will come later. Farther up the angling evolutionary ladder you are easily able to fill all the pockets in the most heavily pocketed vest with the mountains of gear and flies that you feel may be necessary for a day on the water. At some point you realize that you have too much gear in your vest—too many flies, too many gadgets. At this time you also probably have too many rods and reels too, and you begin to realize that you are endangering the simplicity of fly fishing, the quality that first attracted you to it years ago. When you see this simplicity threatened by gear mania, by an overstuffed vest with more pockets than you can use, you begin thinking simplicity. It's ever a challenge because you also want to be prepared for whatever hatches might come off, whatever small emergencies may arise, and you need water, food, rain jacket and so forth. Good luck.

Underneath the vest I nearly always wear a long-sleeve shirt. In the summer, it is a lightweight cotton shirt—old frayed dress shirts work wonderfully. Like the crusty outdoorsmen of the old days said, the best solution to many outdoor problems— such as sun, stickery bushes, poison oak, and mosquitoes—is simply to cover up as much as possible. In the colder weather the shirt will be of wool, and in the really cold weather I'll have a wool sweater on over the wool shirt.

The best angling shirts have two breast pockets with button-down flaps so you can stow more gear—sunglasses, pen, notepad or cigars. The color is not terribly important as long as it is not pink. Much has been written and said about the importance of muted earth tones so as not to visually spook fish. These experts are probably correct, and besides, it seems more reverential toward the river and the natural world to dress in a way that blends with the surroundings, to become one with the flow rather than set yourself apart with colors that are too bold or unnatural.

At least in the West, the well-dressed angler will want to consider wearing a bandana around his neck. While a bandana may seem a decorative frill, it is an immensely useful item. Whether colored red, blue or turquoise, a bandana is the perfect way to keep cool in hot weather by dunking it in the river and tying it around your head under your hat. Or tie it around your neck. If the wind kicks up a dust storm you can place it over your mouth and nose—bandit style—as a dust mask. If you land a large fish, the bandana can be an instant glove enabling you to hold onto the slippery creature. A bandana is part of your first-aid gear and can be used to bind a wound or wrap a sprained ankle. On a day thick with mosquitoes you can soak the bandana with insect repellent and wear it under the back of your hat, hanging down over your neck in the style of the troops in the French Foreign Legion. The bugs stay off your neck and you reduce the amount of repellent that you need to apply directly on your skin.

In all but the hottest summer months you will want a rain and wind jacket with a hood to round out your weatherproof shell. With a good rain parka, waders and warm clothes underneath, it is always surprising how comfortable you can be in foul weather. Because you are wearing waders, your jacket does not have to be cut long, but it should have good cuff closures and a good hood closure. Again, earth tones and dark colors make the best angling jacket colors, as they don't announce your presence to the fish and instead merge with the riparian environment. Anglers have a wide choice of waterproof materials from traditional rubber to nylon to breathable fabrics, depending on your budget. The mark of a well-made jacket is the presence of a large, quality zipper or snaps or both. Nothing is worse on outerwear than small zippers that you can't grip with gloved hands. Also, when zippers malfunction, which they do sometimes, you want snaps as a backup.

In cold weather, gloves will be part of your outfit, too, either traditional wool or neoprene. Except for the coldest weather, I find that the fingerless wool gloves, faced with rubber studs on the palms, are the best hand protection. You can still tie an improved cinch knot with your exposed fingertips, but the rest of your hands stay warm. When wet, the wool still insulates and the rubber studs gives you traction, especially helpful for griping fish or the oar handles of a drift boat.

Of course what really sets the well-dressed angler apart is his hat. Check out black broad-brimmed Pilgrim hats in the illustrations that accompany the better editions of *The Compleat Angler.* Check out the wool tweed caps of more contemporary English salmon anglers, or the fedoras that top anglers' heads from Hemingway's time to our own. A wonderful marriage of form and function, hats come in many shapes and colors and allow an expression of individuality not found with the more utilitarian angling items such as waders and wading boots. Hats perform many functions such as shading your face from the sun, keeping off the rain and protecting your head from low-hanging streamside leaves and branches. A sturdy hat acts as a great bellows on campfires. You can plug the vent holes in the crown and use it as a small bucket for scooping up water. When retiring to the tent at night I turn my hat upside down near me and set my glasses and watch in it so I can find them in the dark. Traditionally, hatbands held flies, but I have never found this a very convenient place to store them.

A respectable angling hat can have a full brim or only a cap brim, but it should not be a convenience store cap with an adjustable plastic band in the back. The best hats are sized, and like a good pair of leather shoes, the hat conforms to the shape of your head and becomes part of you. Of course there are exceptions. For years I wore a cheap cap emblazed with the name of a company that manufactures car oil filters. I wanted to dispel any conception that I might be one of those effete fly-fishers; I cultivated the blue-collar look even though I held a white-collar job.

I've moved beyond that now in my angling evolution and feel free to enjoy the look and feel of a handsome broad-brimmed waxed cotton duck hat. I've never felt comfortable with the English tweed sports-car cap, although they can look great on others. Ditto for the warm-weather visor. I know they are a cool, well-ventilated way of shading the face but they are too California for my tastes, too much of the tennis courts and the links. Head coverings are very personal and likes and dislikes defy explanation. In really hot weather I like a bandana dipped into cold water and tied around my head even though it makes me look like a cross between a Harley-Davidson biker and an aging Grateful Dead hipster. Some anglers—not me— like caps with names of famous fishing lodges, rivers, and fly shops printed on them. In the West, many anglers wear cowboy hats, but I've never felt comfortable with one, always feeling a bit the imposter. As the old-timers say, never wear a hat with more attitude than you can handle.

From a purely practical point of view, it would seem that the broader the brim the better, considering the deleterious effect of the sun on your face, ears and neck. My hat has several inches of brim to it and probably should have more. As for colors, earth tones again. Avoid any of the neon-colored caps that seem so common nowadays but that have no place on the angling waters.

Hat, jacket, waders, boots, the well-outfitted angler is a self-contained unit comfortable in all weathers from dawn to dusk. You shouldn't be distracted by the cold, rain, sleet or sun. The proper gear will take care of that and leave you free to concentrate on getting that Number 14 Parachute Adams into the foam line, just outside the alder branches where the water dimples with trout slurps under an early evening sky.

# V. The Well-Fed Angler

Many are the elements that make a successful fishing camp, the most important, of course, is the fishing. However, often there is little you can do about the fishing: sometimes it's fabulous, other times it's slow and at times it can be rotten. And when it's slow or rotten you can try to improve your angling technique, ascertain what the fish are taking, where the fish are and so forth, but sometimes the bite is simply off. As a local river guide once said, there are two things you can't control on a fishing trip: the fishing and the weather. He concentrated his efforts on what he could control so that even if the fishing was slow and the weather lousy the clients still had a good time.

What you eat at fishing camp is obviously one of those items within your control. Of course, to some anglers, especially the younger, more impatient and energetic anglers, food is simply fuel and its preparation and consumption should be kept to a minimum in order to maximize the time on the water. But to many other anglers, a can of Dinty Moore beef stew at the end of a long fishing day doesn't satisfy. And just as there is room in the river's ecosystem for the otter and the human angler to co-exist, so there is time in the fishing day for angling and for the cooking and eating of good meals. Regardless of the quality of the fishing, the camp food can have a salutary effect on the overall experience: if the fishing and weather are lousy, a well-prepared camp dinner can brighten an otherwise glum day. If the fishing is great and the weather is too, you'll want to celebrate with a fine evening meal.

The importance of good food at fishing camp is a well-established angling tradition. Check out the advertisements for fishing lodges in any magazine, especially the upper-end places. You'll notice attention to the quality of the food right along with the quality of the angling. And it's been this way for years. Walton and his fishing companions dined well on country inn fare, especially on the catch of the day.

"This Trout looks lovely; it was twenty-two inches when it was taken; and the belly of it looked, some part of it as yellow as a marigold, and part of it as white as a lily; and yet methinks it looks better in this good sauce," Walton says.

If you are staying at a lodge, there's little more to be said, as you are not in control of the food preparation. Hopefully, the food will be excellent, and if not, you may think twice about a return visit. Also, if your fishing venture means staying at a motel or cabin there is not a great deal more to say either as you have basically the same conveniences there as you have at home. For our purposes, we are concerned with fishing camps, camps with tents and tarps and propane stoves and wood fires and gas lanterns and plastic coolers filled with ice and food. A fishing camp can be reached by automobile, boat, horse or floatplane, allowing you to take adequate gear and food so that you can cook a wide variety of dishes. A backpacking fishing camp is an altogether different matter, and while you can eat well on a backpack, your selection of food and preparation methods is severely limited.

Cooking at fishing camp is not the same as the regular camp cooking you learned about in Boy Scouts or on family camping trips for one important reason: at fishing camp you don't want to be bending over the Coleman at dusk. You want to be bending over the water taking your number 16 Emerging Caddis out of a large rainbow's jawbone. At least for the fly angler, the best time of the day to fish is what others call dinnertime. To the devoted angler, it's the much anticipated evening rise and you want to be on the water then not lounging about camp drinking a cocktail, tossing greens for a salad or grilling burgers over the coals. To a lesser degree, the same goes for the early morning hours, especially in the hot summer months. You want to be on the water in the cool of the early morning when the insects and fish are active. You don't want to be standing around the campfire, sipping coffee, flipping pancakes.

For you, the camp cook, this means that you will either be cooking dinner early in the day or later at night in the dark. The best solution to this problem I've found over the years is to adapt your eating routine to the time of year you are fishing. In the early summer when the evening rise lingers until 10 o'clock I find a Mediterranean lifestyle works best with angling in the early morning, a large meal in the afternoon, a siesta, an evening's fishing and then a snack before bed. Such a routine was not automatic for me, but evolved in my fishing days after some stubborn early years. Eating dinner at midnight may be romantic in some situations and with certain companions, but it does not aid the digestive system, the sleep process or help you get out of the sleeping bag the next morning at first light.

The other major factor that will determine the type of food you eat at fishing camp will be fire restrictions. In many areas of the West, at least, open fires—even charcoal fires—are not allowed in the summer months thereby restricting your cooking to gas and propane stoves. This limits your camp cooking repertoire, but you can survive quite well, nonetheless.

So, you are on a three-day float trip in June with twilight lingering until 10 o'clock and no open fires allowed. If possible you will fish in the morning and evening and in the middle of the day travel, break camp, set up camp, cook, eat and nap. Depending on your tastes and angling desires, breakfast may be a roll and coffee or it can be more elaborate. Sometimes I like to fish an hour or two in the early morning and then return to camp for a large mid-morning breakfast that in a more urban environment might be called brunch, one of those artificial words that you feel sorry for every time its mangled syllables dribble from your lips.

For a good mid-morning breakfast begin with fresh summer fruit such as cantaloupe wedges and strawberries. Brew some strong coffee. On the Coleman you can use a heavy cast iron pan to first cook a rasher of peppered bacon, filling the air with a distinctive camp aroma. (Do not do this if you are in grizzly country). Wrap the bacon in a paper towel and aluminum foil, drain the pan and fry green onions and parsley in cooking oil and then add the cut-up potatoes. New potatoes work best, either red or white. To hasten the process I usually parboil the potatoes as they cook more quickly than raw potatoes. When the potatoes are just about done, crack in a half-dozen eggs and scramble up a rough equivalent of a Tortilla de Patata a la Espanola, or Spanish omelet.

In place of bacon you might try fresh trout, if the angling regulations allow you to keep a few fish and if you have been lucky. Catch-and-release fishing is a great conservation concept, but it should not be an impediment to enjoying an occasional fish on productive waters that can sustain some consumptive use. Besides, it's good for your angling self to feel fresh fish blood from time to time and to make the flesh of your prey one with your own. Slit open the soft belly with your knife, dissect the stomach for samples of what the fish has been eating, pluck the brilliant red gills from under the gill plates and run your thumb along the exposed backbone cleaning out the blood that always collects there. Wrap the cleaned fish in newspaper, not a plastic bag, and place it next to the ice in the cooler. Later drench the trout in flour, fry in hot oil and serve with lemon slices.

If you have such a large late breakfast you may not want that midday meal until late in the afternoon, right before you begin the evening's fishing. If you did not have such a large breakfast, you might want your midday meal early in the afternoon—a large lunch. Once this meal was called dinner and the evening meal was called supper, but you have to burrow deep into rural America to find those who would use such terms today.

Your choice of meal selections is limited only by your imagination at fishing camp where you have a cooler and a two-burner propane stove. Take a fold-up table to ease the strain on your back. And by all means employ a food box or grub box. My grub box is an old children's wooden toy box with a hinged lid that contains the cast-iron frying pan, two good-sized cooking pots, plates, bowls, cups, utensils, cooking oil, dish soap, salt, pepper and small cutting board. Except for a fresh dishrag and dishtowel, it is always ready to go.

With such a camp kitchen in front of you, you can cook almost anything you cook at home. Several dishes that I cook at fishing camp that are simple and reliable include a salsa meat mix over rice and a chicken and broccoli sauce over noodles.

For the salsa dish, brown burger and a cut-up onion, add a jar of fresh salsa, the type that is refrigerated, and canned corn. Simmer to your satisfaction and serve over rice. When you get tired of tomato-sauce-based dinners, sauté some sliced chicken or pork with onions and garlic, add white wine, cream of mushroom soup, and chicken broth. Simmer and then add cut-up fresh broccoli and cook until the sauce thickens. Serve over warm noodles or rice.

Pasta dishes are always popular at fishing camp and they are not difficult to prepare. The trickiest part can be draining the pasta without a colander. Usually you use the lid of the pot, but be careful to hold it firmly against the rim of the pot so the weight of the pasta and water doesn't push the lid aside when you tip the bottom of the pot upwards to drain the water. Once pasta is spilled on the ground it is difficult to resuscitate. The simplest way to make a pasta dinner is to make a marinara meat sauce at home, bring it in a container in the cooler and heat it while you boil the spaghetti. Serve with some freshly grated Parmesan cheese. Another camp pasta recipe utilizes pesto, chicken and larger noodles such as penne pasta. First, take the pesto out of the cooler to bring it to room temperature. Then slice some chicken breasts into small finger-sized pieces and sauté in olive oil with onions until the chicken is browned and the onions are caramelized. While the chicken is cooking add the penne pasta to boiling water. When the pasta is done, drain the water carefully then add the pesto and chicken to the pot and mix thoroughly. As usual, serve with freshly grated Parmesan cheese.

Now let's consider another fishing trip, another time of year. It is early fall and you are at steelhead camp in a lightly forested area where fires are allowed and it's dark by 6:30 in the evening. You fish until dark, of course, hoping the low light will bring a fish up from the bottom to strike at that Skykomish

Sunrise drifting in the current on a long line. By the time you hike back to camp and get out of your waders it is past seven o'clock. In this camp at this time of year you will want a good gas lantern, hung from a high position to flood the camp kitchen with light. If there are no handy tree limbs around, make a tall tripod with three poles about eight feet long each, tie them together and hang the lantern on top.

You can fire up the Coleman at such a camp and cook what you want, or you can build a fire and grill your dinner. You can't count on a good grill at most campgrounds, and you may not be in a formal campground at all, so you will want to bring a simple steel grill of some kind. Once you have some hot coals, spread out the fire so the flames won't burn the food. A nice touch to a camp grilling fire is to bring along a few fruit wood branches, such as apple or cherry tree prunings from the yard, to flavor the smoke that most likely will be from fir or pine wood.

What should you grill? If you ever eat red meat, now is the time to do so, as steaks never taste better than over a coal fire at camp. Backyard charcoal grilling is good too, but a tender cut of steak, dripping juices into the embers of a night fire in the backcountry awakens the carnivore within. It could be thousands of years ago and you are roasting antelope shanks under a dark sky that is studded with mysterious twinkling dots. These bright dots move in predictable patterns across the sky from season to season. You don't know what the stars are, but you know how they move.

Today, we collectively know a great deal about stars, but few of us know how to track their celestial movements anymore. Though separated from our ancestors by an unimaginable cultural chasm, we are united with them in the ancient enjoyment of fire-roasted fresh meat, a tradition little changed by time or technology. You take a big bite of charred, smoke-scented steak, look away from the fire into the star-filled night sky and think of your angling predecessors with their bone hooks and flint-edged spears. And you think of your graphite rod and high carbon steel hooks and you think of how much has changed and how little has changed, too.

Other grilled favorites include salmon or hatchery steelhead if you have been so fortunate as to have landed one on your trip. I like to wrap the fillet in aluminum foil and cook it until two-thirds done and then open the foil and let the fish pick up the flavor of the smoke and night air. Serve with lemon wedges. Another favorite is corn-on-the-cob. Keep the husks on, dip in water and place on the grill. Rotate the corn on the grill, and when the husks are black the corn is done. Peel back the husks, slather in butter, salt and pepper and enjoy the concentrated flavor of roasted corn.

Another option for a camp where open fires are allowed is a Dutch oven, especially if you don't want to face cooking tasks when you return to camp in the evening. After lunch dig a hole and fill with rocks. (Not river rocks, they might explode). Build a fire in this hole and keep it going for an hour or two to heat up the rocks. In your cast iron Dutch oven assemble a stew with beef or venison or chicken and small whole potatoes and large slices of onions, celery and carrots. (If the potatoes and vegetables are cut into small pieces they will fall apart in the long cooking process). Add seasonings of choice: a bay leaf and tarragon for the chicken stew, for example. Using long-handled tongs pull out several of the rocks. Carefully place the Dutch oven in the hole. Using the tongs, pick up the hot rocks that you set aside and arrange them around the sides and on top of the oven. Fill the hole in with loose dirt and go fishing.

Later in the evening, after you've removed your waders and poured two-fingers of bourbon in your tin cup, go find the spot where you buried the Dutch oven. Hopefully, you have marked it well as it is now dark and you must work by lantern light. I always like to feel the warm earth on top of the buried pot and imagine the stew cooking underneath, steaming and bubbling, alive in its entombment. Also, I always feel a bit like a grave robber, digging into the earth in the black of night by lantern light. You'll want to excavate the site carefully, as you don't want to knock the lid ajar and get dirt in the pot. Fortunately, Dutch oven lids are heavy and fit tightly. Still, I always brush off the seam between the lid and the pot with a paper towel before opening it. What a welcome sight it is to shine a flashlight into a pot that you have dug out of the ground and see a picture-perfect stew bubbling inside: chunks of orange carrots, rich dark crusty pieces of meat and aromatic onions, translucent and collapsed in the dark liquid. It is as though someone else had prepared your meal while you were out fishing. You don't have to fire up the stove and start cooking. All you have to do is eat. Serve with a green salad and crusty French bread for best results. Or if you're really tired, just dig in and forget the salad. Soak up the broth with whatever bread or rolls you have handy. Remember, after dinner when the stew's gone, don't pour cold water into the warm cast iron pot to clean it or it may crack. Have some cookies, smoke a cigar and clean the pot later after it's cooled.

If you don't want to bother digging a hole and filling it with rocks, or if you are in a campground where you are not allowed to dig a hole, you can place the Dutch oven directly in the coals. The coal method cooks the stew in less time. Build a good strong fire of evenly sized wood and wait an hour or so for it to burn down to coals. Then scoop out some of the coals and place the Dutch oven on top of the remaining coals. Remember, when cooking with coals you will need to add more liquid to the stew than when you bury it as steam will escape from the pot during the cooking process despite the weight of the heavy lid. When you bury the oven, virtually no steam escapes and you need less liquid because the released moisture and juices of the meat and vegetables stay in the pot. The stubby legs on the bottom of the oven should elevate the bottom of the pot slightly above the hot coals. Shovel some of the coals that you set to one side on to the top of the flanged lid. Keep a few coals in reserve as you don't want too much heat initially. Later when the heat diminishes you can shovel the saved coals up against the side of the pot. Your stew should be ready in an hour and a half or so, depending on the temperature of the coals. You've got a lot of slack in this type of cooking so you can let it cook longer as the pot will stay warm after the coals have cooled.

Dutch oven, grill or Coleman—you have a variety of methods for cooking at fishing camp. With little effort you can cook excellent food that always tastes better outdoors than at home. Just prior to dinnertime you'll find that the dish of the day becomes the focal point of camp, your companions' appetites stimulated by a few bottles of beer and the aroma of sautéed onions or a tenderloin grilling over the coals. If you are the cook, you will find your companions hovering closer to you the longer the cooking goes on. Nobody wanders off to fish close to dinnertime. The moment before dinner is ready the camp cook is at the apex of his power. Afterwards, when everyone has satiated their hunger they will move on to other things, such as fishing or bed, but for a few moments the cook is king.

And there is something immensely satisfying and civilized about dishing up a good meal in the outdoors and sitting down to enjoy it under the shade of a ponderosa pine or maybe under the cover of a darkening sky, twinkling with evening starlight. Or, if the weather is cold and foul and you have managed to cook a good dinner despite adverse circumstances, the food tastes better yet. A good hot meal served under a makeshift tarp in a rainstorm will revive the spirits of even the most grouchy angler. You go into the country to get away from civilization, to get closer to nature, to act on your ancient predatory urge to fish, and yet a civilized dinner can make your day in a way that nothing else can.

# VI. The Spirited Angler

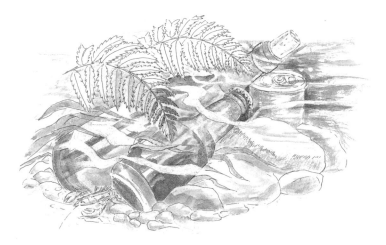

SPIRITED BEVERAGES HAVE BEEN PART OF THE ANGLING tradition since Walton's merry old English characters fortified themselves with draughts of ale. In the early years of the twentieth century, Ernest Hemingway in *The Sun Also Rises* has Jake Barnes and Bill Gorton cool their wine in a spring in the Basque country of northern Spain while they fish for trout in the Irati River. More recently, Norman Maclean in *A River Runs Through It* describes the thirsty angler looking forward to a bottle of Highlander beer chilling in the Big Blackfoot River on a hot day, even though family etiquette does not allow drinking while fishing. But, he adds, "in Montana drinking beer does not count as drinking."

While drunkenness has no place on the angling waters, there is no better place to enjoy an occasional bottle of beer, glass of wine or nip of bourbon than on a fishing trip. More often than not you are in grand surroundings, your streamside camp is in a quiet area, you are with favorite companions and you are filling up the hours of each day with what you truly want to do—fish. The fishing may not be spectacular but it sure beats the alternative of not fishing. And whether the fishing is poor or terrific you'll find time to toast the day with a beverage of your choice.

For most of the angling day, beer and ale are the most appropriate alcoholic beverages. Years ago supplying the beer on a fishing trip was not too complicated, but now with the popularity of the many delicious micro-brews, providing beer on a trip can take some planning. First, remember the bottle opener! Many micro-brews do not have twist-off caps, a fact you often discover after a minute or two of grating your fingers against the fluted edge of the bottle cap. Second, if you are on a raft trip, it may be difficult to take along glass bottles and your selection of canned beer will greatly limit what you bring aboard. All in all, canned beer is much more convenient to take on trips as it packs more efficiently in the ice chest, can be trailed overboard in a mesh bag from a driftboat or raft and the empty cans can be crushed to save space as the trip goes along.

The downside of canned beer is that beer never tastes as good from a can as it does from a bottle, and when you are on the water you don't always have a glass or cup in which to pour the beer. The other disadvantage of canned beer is that when you cool your beer in the river near camp, cans will float away while the heavier glass bottles will stay on the bottom. I know a whitewater rafter who takes very little beer on his trips but counts on retrieving unopened cans of beer that one way or another break away from the other rafting parties.

Personally, I prefer a selection of bottled beer and ale depending on the time of year and the weather. If it is a cold-weather trip I'll take some darker ales such as Porters and bitter ales. You need more sustenance in the cold weather and a light Pilsner doesn't have the backbone to stand up to the frost as does a dark brown Porter with a creamy froth on top. In the warm weather it is just the reverse: the darker ales seem too heavy, languid, not up to the sparkle of the day that is more appropriately marked with a pale ale or traditional Pilsner.

Beer and ale are best consumed cold and keeping such beverages cold on a camping trip requires some planning. The ice chest, of course, is one place to put the beverages, but often it is full of food and other items such as milk that require coldness to prevent spoilage. Chilling your beer is an extra as the beer will not spoil if it isn't cold. But a warm beer on a hot day is little comfort to the hardworking angler so he must make sure to cool his beer one way or another. At your streamside camp you will want to find a slackwater hollow near shore to deposit beer, soft drinks, juice and watermelon. Make sure the current is not so strong as to sweep the bottles and cans away. If you have cans, you might want to keep them in the plastic six-pack ring and slip the plastic holder over the end of a branch to anchor it.

When, during the angling day, you open a bottle of beer or ale is your decision and rests largely on your fishing schedule. Charles Cotton, who wrote the fly fishing section for the fifth edition of *The Compleat Angler*, liked to start the day with a drought of ale as soon as he was dressed and not another glass until lunch. If you are up at dawn and fish the morning hard you may want a latemorning beer prior to the large late breakfast you are cooking. On a summer's late morning, when the sunrise chill is fast changing to the heat of the day, a cold beer absolutely is on the mark. You'll want a light ale or Pilsner at this hour and if possible you will want to pour it into a glass or cup to allow the gases to escape. If this isn't possible, you can gently shake the bottle once you have taken a sip or two and allow a head to develop inside.

After a cold beer you'll want to wolf down the eggs, potatoes and bacon you have cooked. Stuffed, relaxed and needing a midday breather, you will search for a shady spot under the alder tree. Place your sleeping pad down on the long grass, or better yet take along a lightweight portable hammock that you can string between two trees. Take a load off, tilt your hat over your eyes, swing in the breeze, in the shade, and have the nap you deserve in preparation for the afternoon's angling.

If you are on a boat trip you might drink a bottle of beer as you float along. If you're in serious white water, the oarsman will want to refrain from imbibing, just as you would not drink and drive a car. Otherwise, it is hard to imagine a finer spot to enjoy a favorite beer or ale than from the seat of a driftboat as it slowly snakes down a trout river. A booth at the best pub in London would not compete with your driftboat seat, neither would the best window seat at any of the swank cocktail lounges that occupy the top floors of many American skyscrapers. The river current moves you along at its pace, sometimes in no hurry at all and at other times swiftly through the chutes and around the midstream islands flanked by broad gravel bars. You are part of the snowmelt from the distant mountains that is bound for the salt, a cold, clean aqua-green colored column of water that defines the country it drains. You watch the fish rises along the alder-choked bank, dimples on the river's smooth skin, noisy slurps in the quiet of the day, a day spent far from internal combustion engines, telephones and freeway traffic. You hear the chatter of the current rushing across a gravel bar and spot a great blue heron standing in the shallows watching for fish winks in the drift. Mid-afternoon caddis flutter by and you try unsuccessfully to catch one in the air. Then you notice a few climbing on the gunwale and you dig into your fly boxes to match the hatch. If it's hot you undo your bandana and dip it in the cold river water and wrap it around your neck or head. Dip your hat in too and anchor its wet coolness on your head. It's best to keep your beer bottle out of the sun if you can, as it will heat up quickly on a summer day mid-stream. Use a Styrofoam cupholder.

Later in the day before dinner is another time to have a bottle or two of beer. Especially in the hot weather, there is no beverage that can slack a tired angler's thirst like a cold beer: not sweet, slightly bitter, its effervescence light and refreshing for a parched mouth and throat. On these hot afternoons, after you have hooked a few large rainbows in the back eddies on small Elk Hair Caddis, and after you have walked back to camp along a hot and dusty trail flanked by sunburnt cheat grass and dry brittle tumbleweeds, then when you arrive at camp you head for the cooler, the opener and the hammock in the shade. This is a time of great satisfaction in the angling day, as you do absolutely nothing for awhile: no casting, wading, rigging gear or camp chores. You swing gently in the hammock, as lazy as you can be. You rest those weary back and leg muscles that have fought the current all day long, and you ruminate on your fishing success or lack thereof. The cold tingle of the beer in your mouth satisfies the palate and heartens the angling soul. Later, after you are rested, you vacate the hammock and begin fixing dinner, and yes, another bottle of beer will go well with your food preparation duties.

When dinner arrives, you often think of wine, and if you haven't had too much beer, a glass of wine can go nicely with dinner. At the risk of offending wine connoisseurs, I would generally not recommend white wine on the river. For my taste buds, most white wines are awfully light on body. And the ones that are good are too good, too smooth, so smooth that they go down too easily. You don't realize that you already are on your third glass and you'll pay for it the next morning. Red wines are another matter, and a strong claret or Chianti on the river with a dinner that has a tomato sauce or red meat can be perfect. The stronger acid taste and fuller body forces you to sip it slowly, like eating a single piece of dark German rye bread compared to eating half a loaf of Wonder bread.

A good dry red wine sipped streamside tastes especially rich, reminiscent of crushed ripe grapes, sunny vineyards and the pungent aroma of harvest time in wine country. Too often we associate fine wines with fancy restaurants and the outdoors is relegated to the canned beer and half-gallon whiskey crowd. Not so. As with everything you drink or eat outside, wine tastes better outdoors. You think of the grapes that are the raw material of your drink and they seem far away from the stream you are on, from a distant land of softly sloping hillsides laced together with row upon row of gnarled grapevines. A cup of wine—leave the stem-wear at home—with dinner civilizes your outdoor dinner and in turn civilizes you.

Before or after dinner, or around the campfire late at night, you might want some stronger spirits. Here again, the fresh air and scent of juniper, pine and sage enhances the flavor of whatever you drink. In the hot weather a gin and tonic before dinner—in a plastic glass or tin cup—provides a biting coolness to the day's heat. Gather a few ice chips from the ice bag in the cooler and put them in a cup. Slice a lime and pull the bottle of tonic water from the river hollow. Squeeze the juice from a wedge of lime into the cup and drop the wrung-out wedge into the cup as well. Add a jigger of gin and then top off with tonic water. Let the drink sit a few minutes so the ice has time to chill the liquid. The gin, ice, lime and tonic mix to form a hot-weather drink that can't be beat and that seems exotic in a camp setting. You expect one of these at home on the deck after a tough day at the office in August, but streamside it seems especially good.

In most other weather, and even in hot weather, whiskey has a powerful appeal in the outdoors. I'm not sure why this is so, but sipping a good bourbon in a camp chair where you can watch the river flow by or in front of an evening campfire can be deeply satisfying. The strong, warm whiskey taste is clearly a human-made artifact in this natural world of water and rock and vegetation. It contrasts sharply with the natural-ness around you. While some rotting wild apples might fer-ment and crudely resemble the fermentation of beer or wine, nothing in nature can reach the distilled essence of a fine bourbon. The flavor of bourbon is far removed from its natur-al ingredients—it doesn't taste like grain anymore as wine still tastes of grapes; it has the flavor of copper tubing and charred oak barrels. Its origins are natural but it has become a cultural product, just as a painting is more than the earthen pigments and the cotton canvas that it is painted upon. Whiskey stings the tongue and warms the throat unlike anything else. Strong spirits are one of the characteristics that separate men from beasts. Animals drink water as we do, and may even taste fer-mented fruit on occasion when they feed on rotting apples or berries, but you won't find anything akin to bourbon in nature.

While I like my bourbon neat, or with an ice cube or two, I don't like it warm so in hot weather if you don't have any ice to spare you can keep the bottle in the cooler or in the stream. Putting the whiskey bottle directly in the cooler is something I learned from antelope hunters who pursue pronghorn in the high-desert country of the West in late August. Camped in this spare, nearly treeless country under a blistering daytime sun, ice is a rare commodity that can't be chipped away to put into drinks. The hunters learned that if they wanted their spirits cool they would have to place the bottle next to the ice and not put the ice in the drink itself.

Much has been said in outdoor literature about whiskey from a tin cup and most of it is true. It tastes better that way. Maybe the alcohol leaches out trace metals in the tin cup, metals that we crave. Whatever it is, the special tang of whiskey swirled about a metal cup is unmistakable. With that said, my camp gear contains more plastic cups than metal ones. Call me untraditional, but I find the plastic cups more practical around camp. In the morning, metal cups heat up when full of coffee and by the time you can press your lips against them the coffee is lukewarm. In the evening, the cups are warm with the heat of the day and all too quickly heat up the bourbon that you painstakingly cooled in the cooler or the stream.

Plastic or tin, whatever the cup, I prefer to fill it with bourbon rather than Scotch, though I have nothing against these whiskeys from across the Atlantic. I prefer the robustness and deeper coloration of bourbon. Besides, I think we Americans tend to undervalue what we have here at home and search in vain for cultural sophistication overseas. I like the idea that a decade ago a fourth-generation Kentucky woodsman labored under a bright Appalachian sun to funnel his brew—made with iron-free limestone cave water—into barrels made of local oak. And I like the names on the bottles, all American, all real: Wild Turkey, Rebel Yell, Henry Clay, Jack Daniels, Old Heritage, Elijah Craig, Old Grand Dad, Old Rip Van Winkle, Eagle Rare. Like the Scotches, you can get your bourbons at any quality you can afford from the blends to the top of the line single barrel bottlings.

Moderation in all matters of the spirits should be the watchword in fishing camp, for we are anglers, not party-time whitewater rafters or conventioneers. You've got to get up early in the morning and get that big black stonefly nymph in the pocketwater just downstream of camp when the really large fish will be working. You don't want to wake up with a pounding headache and a mouth that feels like a place where spiders crawled into and died. If you don't feel good in the morning, you won't feel good all day. You want to savor each day on the water and not squander your time hungover like a college fresh-man away from home for the first time. Forget the extra night-cap. With all the wading, casting, walking and rowing you did during the day, and the cool fresh night air, you'll get to sleep soon enough.

# VII. THE NATURALIST ANGLER

FOR MANY, THE NATURAL WORLD HAS BECOME A DISTANT, faint, almost forgotten force in the post-industrial universe of the Second Millennium. It has become increasingly rare for most of us to notice the workings of the natural world anymore because we are so far removed from the seasons, the weather, the interplay among the many life forms on the food chain. In our urban environments we go about our daily business largely oblivious to natural conditions: our homes, office towers, shopping malls, factories and automobiles are all climate controlled. We are shielded at every turn from cold, heat, rain, wind, fog and sleet. The thermostat is our best friend. In many parts of the country there are only a few weeks a year when it is not turned on: either for heating or cooling. The weather has proven more difficult to control than the temperature, so we have moved more and more of our activities indoors. You go inside immense, sprawling malls to shop, in contrast to the past when you walked on sidewalks from store to store. You go inside huge domed arenas to watch sporting events such as baseball and football that once were played outside. We have done our best to hide from the weather, to avoid its inconveniences, its discomforts. Only now and then do winter blizzards, summer heat waves or hurricanes remind us of the natural forces around us. The rest of the time our lives go on like clockwork regardless of the weather. And our separation from the natural world goes on and on for we no longer need to live in places with ample water or arable land. We can live comfortably in the middle of inhospitable deserts, such as the hundreds of thousands of people who crowd Las Vegas every day. Archaeologists tell us that civilization began in the Fertile Crescent. Now our culture flourishes wherever— fertile or infertile—oblivious to the natural surroundings, discombobulated, distanced, apart from the biological fundamentals of sun, soil and water. It is not far-fetched to imagine that we could live on the moon given our ability to divorce ourselves from the environment around us.

When you go fishing you leave all this behind. You reconnect to the natural world. You are not only outside, you are outdoors. To go outside is to walk out onto the deck or into the backyard; to go outdoors is to travel farther. When you're outdoors, the weather is no longer a distant force that can be easily neutered. If you have spent much time on the angling waters you have likely seen nature in her many moods from blowing snow to summer's heat. While you need to pay attention to the weather, and dress properly for it, it becomes after awhile something that is wondrous in its variety, a wonder that you don't appreciate in a climate-controlled indoor life. Sun, snow, rain, wind and fog infuse the fishing landscape with another dimension.

There are times, of course, when the conditions are ideal and it appears as though there is no weather at all. But then the weather closes in and you submit to a force higher than yourself. Once on a late-spring fishing trip, what had been a day of pleasant weather began changing in the late afternoon. The wind gusted, dust devils funneled skyward, raced a few hundred yards twisting along the banks and then disappeared. Another gust would come along and more twisting dust funnels would spiral up the slopes. Face into a gust and you could scent the changing atmosphere charged with a different voltage than before.

We had not been at our camp long and we were relaxing in folding chairs, resting before beginning our dinner preparations, anticipating the evening rise. But the gathering storm could not be ignored. Your senses told you in many ways that a thunderstorm was coming: you could feel it, smell it and see it. Above the rust-brown rimrock horizon the sky was changing minute by minute, like time-lapse cinematography. But today there was no artificial screen membrane or contrived time separating us from the darkening sky that minutes ago was a light-blue color, patched with high, fluffy cumulus clouds. Usually, thunderstorms in this desert country are preceded by a gradual buildup of thick rolling cumulus clouds. But this time they amassed at once, it seemed, a solid dark gray underbelly of suspended moisture. You could look over your shoulder toward the northeast and see the cumulonimbus coming, dimming the late-afternoon sunlight with their massive blackness. This was unusual too as generally the weather in this area comes in from the southwest. The heavy, darkening northeast sky pressed down on the crew-topped basalt mesa.

"We might want to get the tents up," I said to Chris and Mike. They had been thinking the same thing and we worked quickly for the weather was changing by the minute.

The ripcord-connected aluminum poles slid together easily. We placed the end of each pole in a brass grommet at the base of the tent and under tension the long pole transformed into an arch as we slid the other end of the pole into the grommet at the opposite side of the tent. Three such arches criss-crossed one another providing the exterior frame for our thin nylon shelter. We snapped the plastic clips on the top of the tent onto the poles. Next came the rain fly, which we snapped on hurriedly. I found a grapefruit-sized basalt rock and hammered in tent stakes. Mike guyed down the fly in a few places, tying the guys off on large rocks with long loops in the cord. We collected our gear into a central mass and threw a plastic tarp over the top and weighted in down with sticks and rocks. Then we burrowed into the tents: Mike and I into the larger one and Chris into his small tent.

Thunder clapped up in the rimrock, still a ways off, and a few raindrops began to fall. The usually blue desert sky was as dark as I have ever seen it in daytime. Had there been streetlights about, they probably would have come on. The temperature dropped and the humidity rose. A flash of lightning.

"One-thousand one, one-thousand two, one-thousand three...." I counted. Another clap of thunder and it was closer than before. The canyon walls were nearly lost in the dark clouds that hung down into the river gorge, far below their usual elevation, distended with moisture, no longer distant puffs against a hot, pale-blue sky, but in your face, moving like dirty fog down the slopes all the way to the river, fusing the river of the sky with the river of the earth. Cloud water, river water, a world of water on a parched landscape of sand, sagebrush, juniper and rock. The rain came hard and it was good to be in a tent looking out through the door, sheltered, protected from the force that suddenly had turned the daytime dark. The rain pelted the tent; the wind shook the guys. The fly puffed and bellowed in the strong gusts and we thought it might tear, but it held.

Another flash brightened the sky. Mike and I looked at each other inside the tent where we were comfortably reclining on our sleeping pads. He had an expectant look on his face, and I probably did too. We both knew without saying a word that the lightning signaled the beginning of something, not the end.

"KA-BOOM!"

The thunder exploded before you could say "one-thousand one." We not only heard this one, we felt it, rumbling through the air, through our inconsequential flesh into the greater density of the earth underfoot to be absorbed without a murmur: an angry Zeus hurling thunderbolts, Thor swinging his magic hammer, the Thunderbird flying through the sky leaving a trail of thunder eggs across the land, drab-colored round nodules that house a brilliant quartz interior. Whoever your thunder god is, you think of him when you are in a tent wondering if aluminum poles attract electricity and where the voltage will go if it finds the tent—into you or into the ground. At least you are not standing foolishly in the water waving a long graphite stick around at this moment. And you understand why your distant ancestors invented thunder gods to account for this sudden natural violence. They had no idea why the usually quiet sky flashed with lightning and roared with the terrifying sound of thunder. They had no way of knowing that lightning is only a bright flash caused by the discharge of atmospheric electricity between clouds or between the clouds and earth. They didn't know that this electrical discharge heats and expands the air causing the thunderclap. You know all this, of course, as a modern man, a scientific man, and still the thunder is frightening.

The eastern horizon flashed again with more lightning. I counted again and this time got to one thousand four before the thunder rolled, and I knew that the storm was moving away. We talked awhile and soon noticed that the rain no longer pounded as hard on the tent as it did minutes before and the fly had stopped flapping. Like an emerging caddis, I crawled out of the tent and surveyed the camp and all was as it was before, except an upturned corner of the tarp covering our gear that was blown loose by the wind. To the south the storm was still unleashing itself on the land, but here the air was still, freshened by the rain that settled the dust. The sun broke out from behind the clouds and daytime never seemed so bright.

"What a storm," I said to Chris who was getting out of his tent, too. I walked over to the cooler, took out a bottle of beer and started dinner preparations.

A storm forces you to notice the natural world at work, but most of the time when you are fishing the forces of the nature act in more subtle ways. How much of the natural world you absorb while fishing depends on your powers of observation. The naturalist angler could also be called the observant angler for the best anglers are keenly observant people. The power of observation is part learned, part natural and increasingly in short supply in our hurried world. In our everyday lives we spend very little time observing anything, much less the workings of the natural world. Our daily patterns propel us to stay busy with work tasks and home chores, one piled upon the other. In the few moments when you are not busy you are to be entertained by television, a movie or go to a theme park. To sit alongside a riverbank and observe the flow of the current, watch the insects hatch and listen to the birds sing is to be a time-wasting derelict.

Some of the best anglers I know do exactly that when they get to a new piece of water: they sit down and study the flow before they start fishing. They let the river speak to them. It doesn't take long, maybe ten to fifteen minutes, but in that brief time you might observe rising fish, cruising fish just under the surface, silver winks in the riffle water. You might observe insects in the air, the wind blowing grasshoppers into the edge water, recently shucked exoskeletons on the streamside rocks. And you might assess the level of the flow, whether the river appears to have risen or fallen recently by the signs along the bank. You might spot likely looking feeding spots along the current seams and in the fast-water slicks. You might notice the foam lines, the slant of the sun, the direction of the wind.

The best anglers observe this and more when they "read" the water, one of the most descriptive phrases in the angling lexicon. The rest of us, when we reach a good-looking fishing spot, struggle with the impulse to start fishing immediately. When you see a nice piece of water you want to get going; it's frustrating to wait and watch, like the heron standing in the shallows, whisper still, not moving at all. It stands for long minutes, tens of minutes, looking, watching, pinpoint focused in a way incomprehensible to your wandering mind. Then when you think it must be asleep, its long neck plunges toward the water in a flash and it spears a small fish and swallows it whole. At times you have the heron's patience and wait and watch, and at other times you find yourself all too human and plow into the water minutes after you arrive on the scene. I excuse myself for the times when I am too eager and forge ahead without sufficient observation with the excuse that, after all, I am only a human predator and lack the animal predator's concentration. If my daily meal depended on my stealth, then maybe I'd be more patient.

Walton was a keen observer and an early naturalist angler. His knowledge of fish and their habits and foods is remarkable considering the lack of scientific study on this subject at the time he wrote, two centuries before Darwin developed his theory of evolution. Walton includes observation, along with diligence and practice, as essential characteristics for the successful angler. Consider the care he advises when approaching a piece of water:

"And before you begin to angle, cast to have the wind on your back, and the sun, if it shines, to be before you, and to fish down the stream; and carry the point or top of your rod downward, by which means the shadow of yourself, and rod too, will be the least offensive to the fish; for the sight of any shade amazes the fish, and spoils your sport, of which you must take a great care," Walton says.

The observant angler develops into the naturalist angler by expanding his observations slowly from the initial point of interest, the fish, to the fish's food, the type of water conditions fish favor, the riparian zone, the uplands, the watershed, and the great hydrological cycle that makes life possible for the fish and the fisherman. You don't think of all these things at once as it would be too overwhelming. Instead, you begin with your prey—the fish. As a fisherman, you likely know more about fish than ninety-five percent of the general population, making a slim allowance for the handful of ichthyologists who know more than anyone.

The observant angler can spot fish in a river and tell you what they are doing. His first accomplishment is simply seeing them. I have been fishing a number of times with my angling mentor Bill from Portland when he has seen steelhead in streams where I see nothing but rocks. Even when I put on Polarized sunglasses and can see through the reflective glare of the water surface I have problems. One thing I learned early on from Bill, and a few others, was not to look for fish when looking for fish. Look for suggestions of fish, movements in the water that might be fish, bright flashes that might be fish. I learned the same thing from veteran deer hunters, such as my friend Michael, who spend long hours searching for deer, never expecting to see a full-bodied deer standing in the middle of an open field. The accomplished deer hunter looks for a patch of deer hair contrasting in color or shape to the surrounding brush, a movement in an otherwise still landscape, an antler tine sparkling in the sun.

You will not likely, at least at first glance, see the entire body of a fish as large as a steelhead. You will see a portion of the fish, a bright flash, some movement among the rocks, a dark oval shape slowly undulating in the flow. Fish such as steelhead and trout are colored dark on top so that they blend into the color of the river bottom when seen from above. You learn to look for this dark shape. If you can get up on a steep bank your angle of vision will be more direct with less surface glare. You learn to be patient when sighting fish as the skin of the water is ever changing: one minute it is like a mirror and you can't penetrate the surface glare at all. The next minute the light shifts and you can see six feet straight down to the cobble on the bottom.

Seeing the fish is only the beginning if you are seeking trout. The experts want to find not only trout, but feeding trout. I'm told that when you spot a trout you are supposed to notice if it is lying on the bottom or suspended in the water column. Look for a shadow on the river bottom to tell if it is suspended. If it is suspended, and moving a little from side to side, it is a feeding fish and you are in business. If it is lying on the bottom without a shadow it is a resting fish and you will have a difficult time persuading it to strike at your offering.

I admire the disciplined, observant anglers who can, in actual field conditions, really notice such things and put such findings to use. I have struggled for years to be able to tell if rising fish are rising to adult insects or if they are taking emerging pupae. A splashing rise means they are taking adults; a dimpled rise means pupae, or so the conventional wisdom goes. In practice, on the river in all types of light, water and weather conditions, none of this is easy.

Some observant anglers concentrate not on how and what they see, but how the fish sees, what the fish sees. They claim that fish are what we humans would call near sighted: their vision is sharp up close, but not so good far away. They claim that when fish are feeding they focus only on the food floating by in front of their noses. If you are quiet, you can walk right up to them at such moments, the experts say.

The observations of anglers about fish and their habits could go on and on. Some of it is probably true, too. The next level of observation most anglers attend to after they learn something about their quarry, is their quarry's quarry. To understand fish is to know that they need different types of water in which to feed, rest and seek protection from predators. They also need food. All creatures in the animal kingdom eat or are eaten, depending on their place on the food chain. Nature is a violent place, not a bucolic one, and the prospect of sudden death is an everyday reality. Those of us at the top of the food chain sometimes think the natural world is benign only because another animal is not lurking nearby ready to pounce upon us. Spend some time in grizzly country where you are not on top of the food chain and it will change your orientation toward nature.

Anyway, the observant angler usually turns his attention from his prey to his prey's prey after awhile. Fish eat other fish, leeches, mice, frogs, fish eggs, grubs, crabs, shrimp and insects of all kinds. All anglers who want a fish to strike at what they offer on the end of their line pay attention to the eating habits of fish. The attention to fish food assumes its highest form among the fly-anglers who over the years have learned and passed on a wealth of knowledge about aquatic insects. Almost no one other than fly-fishermen and entomologists understand the rudimentary life history of aquatic insects: that they live under water, get oxygen through gills just as fish do, metamorphose and turn into creatures of the land that obtain oxygen from the air. Since Walton's time, anglers especially fly-anglers, have made a detailed study of this and we have more information at our disposal on this subject than we can absorb today.

This wealth of information about caddisflies, mayflies, stoneflies, midges, terrestrial insects and others is the subject of many volumes nowadays. What is especially fascinating about this information on fish food, however, is how anglers have put it to use. At first, anglers simply put the larvae or adult flies on a hook and used it as bait, as Walton did with cased caddis larvae which he claims can be preserved for two to three weeks in a bait box. Later anglers developed hundreds of ways of attaching feathers, hair and fur to hooks to imitate the various stages of aquatic insects.

To continue on the subject of fly-tying or entomology would be to repeat what has been said by many others who actually know something about the subject. The observant angler is part born and part bred, and some of us seem born to absorb only so much. Just as in school or on the job, some things stick and others do not. Some of us remember historical dates easily, lyrics of popular songs easily, or how to calculate price-to-earnings ratios easily. Some people actually remember the definition of the Doppler effect. I don't consider myself an unobservant angler, but at the same time my concentration begins to falter at a certain point on the insect taxonomy charts. I know I should continue, go deeper, learn more. Maybe one day I will; it would help my fishing success. Those who truly understand the hatches and how to imitate them catch more fish. But we all reach our limits. The observant angler can become a naturalist, but he or she does not have to become an entomologist. A naturalist studies the physical world in its wholeness and in a non-technical manner. The naturalist was at his apex several centuries ago, before the study of the natural world evolved into its many rigorous disciplines that in turn relegated the naturalist to amateur status.

The observant angler takes time to look up from his microscopic study of fish and the fish's food to the larger habitat that the fish lives in: the water and rocks of the river, the streamside vegetation that shelters and frames the river, the uplands that drain into the river, the distant mountains and the clouds in the sky that are the source of our rivers. To be an angler is to know a variety of waters from the salt to the glacier rivulets. The ocean is a good starting point because that is where fish life began millions of years ago and it is the destination of the freshwater streams and creeks and rivers that drain our landscape. To understand the workings of the natural world, as the naturalist angler learns to understand, is to know the primacy of the Great Salt. Here in this immense saline solution is the birthplace and final resting place of our freshwater streams. The atlas tells us that ninety-seven percent of the water on the earth is salt water. These great oceans, seas, gulfs, sounds and bays cover seventy-one percent of the earth's surface. Even if you do not fish in salt water you are connected to it, hydrologically connected. Even you, the Colorado trout angler more than a thousand miles from either ocean who has never wetted a line in salt water, never fished for anadromous fish and could care less about the salt, you are connected to the salt, for without the oceans the life-giving hydrological cycle would cease. Yes, some of our rainfall comes from clouds that form over the land, but more water falls on the land than evaporates from the land and the difference is made up in the Great Salt.

There on the ocean's swells, water is constantly evaporating, the moist air rising and expanding as it encounters less pressure at higher altitudes. As the air rises and expands it cools into tiny water droplets or ice crystals and forms clouds, the progenitors of our rivers: layered altostratus, thinly veiled cirrostratus and puffy, pillowed cumulus. They float along, some like ragged blimps with dark pregnant undersides ripe with condensation, others bright and white with no outward sign of the water vapor within, all of them pushed about in the sky by breezes, storms, trade winds. And when these drifting water sacks eventually reach their saturation point it rains. Or it snows, or sleets or hails. Moisture that was once in the ocean has been transported into the air and moved great distances in the sky by the ethereal workings of the atmosphere: sun, air, earth and water all intertwined, interconnected in the hydrological cycle.

This moisture from the clouds is the beginning of the rivers and the fish and the insects and the life of the waters. In my part of the country, much of this precipitation comes down as snow in the mountains so that the sources of rivers are most often to be found above the timberline, in the snowpack that covers the alpine meadows for most of the year. The very beginnings of things are always fascinating, and it is always a pleasure to be high in the mountains and step across a tiny rivulet emerging from under a snowbank. There are no fish here, of course, but in my mind I'm still fishing when I'm here at the beginning, seeing, hearing, touching and drinking the source of the fish's primary element—water. In the summer I like to hike high into the mountains above the treeline along a sharp divide and watch the snowmelt rivulets flow into different watersheds. Those of us who love rivers are drawn to their sources, just as you desire to know the source of many things, some of which you will know the source of and others that you will not. With rivers you can find the source if you spend some time in the mountains, and it gives you a feeling of greater intimacy with a river afterwards to be able to say that you know its fount.

At the top of a large mountain you look down on many watersheds. That's why it is so easy to lose your way on the descent when mountain climbing. Drainages converge at the summit into a pinpoint, but they widen as you glissade downhill. Fifty feet of horizontal difference at the peak becomes miles apart at the mountain's base. On top of my home mountain, the 11,235-foot Mt. Hood in Oregon's Cascade Range, the snow-covered peak drains into many streams and rivers and watersheds. Turn around in the thin air at the top, the wind roaring in your face and the ultraviolet light blistering your lips, and you look down through your dark glasses at watersheds in every direction.

Up high on mountains such as those in the Cascade Range, you walk on remnants of the last ice age, shrunken glaciers clinging to the high-elevation slopes. Glaciers always add a sense of history to rivers as the melt from them—the thick chalky glacier melt—is not from last winter's snowfall but from ice that formed thousands of years ago. The Sandy Glacier, Zigzag Glacier, White River Glacier, Eliot Glacier, Coe Glacier all ring Mt. Hood with a reminder of times past. They invest the mountain-born, youthful rivers with age, with Pleistocene water that until yesterday was frozen in time. In the late summer, after the fresh snowpack is gone, this milky Stone Age glacier water fills the spry little streams, and when it does you usually take your fishing rod elsewhere. Visibility contracts to less than an inch in a glacier-melt stream making angling nearly impossible.

However, as in all things angling, the nearly impossible can at times become possible. I once successfully fished a glacier-melt river and caught several fine silver salmon in water the color of concrete. It was on the Kustatan River less than an hour's flying time southwest of Anchorage. Our pilot, Joe Phillips, put us down on the windswept tundra and parked his small, fixed wheeled craft alongside several other light planes. As in much of Alaskan fishing, you arrived at this river by plane or a long hike, as it was far from any road. About a mile down-stream of where we were to fish, the river flowed into the broad mudflats of Cook Inlet. We were to fish for incoming silvers on the high tide, which today was not high at all by Alaskan standards, only twenty-two feet. I started to uncase my fly rod, but a look at the river the color concrete changed my mind. A fish couldn't see a fly if one hit it on the nose. Everyone else was fishing by scent and so did I.

"Where's that spin rod?" I asked Leo. Soon I had the spin rod setup in hand and put on the terminal tackle consisting of an ounce and one half of lead and a knuckle-sized glob of salmon roe.

Just like clockwork at high tide the run came in, hidden in the dirty water but there, finning their way upstream away from the salt toward their freshwater breeding grounds. The four anglers in our party landed fourteen silvers in less than two hours, maybe less than an hour. I can't remember. What I do remember is the surprise of fish taking the bait in the off-color water, water so milky that when you dunked your hand in the flow it disappeared from view. Yet you'd cast out into the river, let the roe swing in the current and you'd get a strike, the fish apparently locating your bait by scent. Soon, the tide began to ebb and so did the fishing.

"Let's get going," said Joe. He searched the broad, flat tree-less expanse nervously, concerned that the smell of fresh fish on the bank might attract grizzlies. Once, he told me, a party on another Alaskan river stored several salmon in their plane and then went back to fishing. A grizzly smelled the fish and dug right through the fuselage to get at them. Joe wanted to keep his plane intact, so we gathered our silvers and tackle and taxied down the improvised dirt runway.

Back in the lower 48, on the slopes of Mt. Hood, the glaci-er melt, snowmelt, rainfall and seeps etch the hillsides with hundreds of tiny rivulets, drawing water off the land like veins collecting blood under your skin. Gravity draws the water down into ever wider and deeper creeks and streams and finally rivers. Along the way the flow is often arrested in ponds and lakes where the water rests, settles and then continues its journey through the outlet down the next slope. Moving water is hypnotic: the stream angler is easily mesmerized by its flow, its interplay with the rock riverbed and the brushy banks. And he learns a great deal about the interplay of water and rock in his time on the river. The hydrologist and geologist know more about this phenomenon, but the angler is not far behind in understanding the relation between rocks and water. You learn from fishing to study the banks so as to understand the riverbed contours underneath. If the bank is steep with big rocks, then the riverbed probably has steep sides with big rocks. That slick in the middle of the riffle is probably a trench where fish rest, seeking a break from the current. You learn about the relationship between the water and the fish, where fish rest, where they spawn and where they feed. You learn on every river the pattern of riffles, pools, runs, drifts, eddies and slots. There is an infinite variety to moving water; every stream, creek and river is as different from one another as we are from one another. And you marvel at the power of water, that such a soft substance can cut through hard rock, move it, mold it and grind it into sand.

One reason many fly-anglers get to know rivers so well is that they spend a lot of time immersed in them, wading in water that may be ankle deep or chest deep. You become more intimate with a river when you are in it and of it, as opposed to floating on it in a boat or standing on its banks. When you are wading a stretch of water you see a lot of the life of the river that you otherwise might miss. Standing still in the water, waist deep and quiet, I have had ducks swim within a few feet of me, unsuspecting and unaware of my presence. I have stood absolutely still while a river otter swam between the bank and me four feet away.

You realize how quiet a place nature is when you are wading a lonely piece of water, how far we have wandered from that natural quiet with our freeway noise, jackhammers and leaf blowers. All you hear on the river is the splash of water against rocks, the hum of gravity pulling water to the sea. At first your ears ring and it all seems empty and you feel alone for the want of the usual background noises. But before long you become accustomed to it and grow quieter yourself. But just as you settle into the quiet rhythm of the natural world, the river may startle you, for nature is not always a quiet place. I remember once fishing on a mid-stream gravel bar for a half hour or more with no one else around—dead quiet except for the sound of running water tripping over the rocks.

WACK!

I nearly jumped out of my waders. I turned around and saw a beaver swimming downstream right behind me. Apparently, it had seen me and slapped its broad tail on the water in alarm. We were both surprised by each other's presence, but I believe I was the more startled.

And there was the time I was wading hard up against a tall grassy bank and casting out into the current. The rod tip touched the top of the tall grasses behind me on the back cast and suddenly an angry, cackling rooster pheasant exploded into the air, flew upslope in flurry of wing beats and then disappeared from view leaving me shaken once again. These things happen to you when you are wading.

Farther down along the river, as it deepens, merges with other rivers and becomes wider than a quick canoe paddle across, you will leave your waders behind and either fish from the bank or a boat. By now the river is in its middle years, moving toward old age, if you subscribe to the notion that a river's journey is not unlike our own. The youthful creeks flow fast and wild down the mountain slopes. As the gradient flattens rivers slow, widen and deepen into middle age. And as they mature into old-age, rivers flatten more and eventually become tidal, pushing their freshwater plume out into the ocean where all the waters of the land intermingle and become one. When a river broadens beyond your ability to shout across it and be heard on the other side, then the dynamics of the river bottom and the water itself become of greater concern to the angler than does the shape of the bank. There is less interplay between the structure of the bank and the moving water, and most of the water is flowing far from any bank. There are no more rapids or boulders breaking the water's surface, no white water, no riffles, no chop. You are still fishing moving water, but it is slick water, flat water, water moving under a smooth unwrinkled skin.

And flat water it remains all the way to the ocean, for the world of riffles, boulders, pockets, snags, sweepers and cutbanks belongs to the upstream rivers on the steeper slopes where gravity tugs harder on the flow. From the big rivers to the saltwater bays, the world of flat water presents a different angling challenge. To the angler accustomed to smaller rivers with instream structure, grassy banks, pockets, and clattering riffles, the world of flat water is a new experience. Like the observant stream angler who can differentiate between resting fish and feeding fish, the observant flatwater angler notices things that others do not. On a charter salmon-fishing trip once off the Oregon coast our captain looked for changes in the water's color, where the deep blue took on a greenish tint. He looked for foam lines, feeding birds and other signs of rip currents that might concentrate baitfish and in turn salmon. He watched his depth gauge and other instruments and it was a whole new type of fishing, far removed from casting a PMD under the alder branches of a bouldered stream. The naturalist angler cannot know all things on all waters, as the world of fishing is too large to be familiar with it all, but he learns to appreciate those who know how to read the water in its many languages.

Unlike the freshwater angler struggling to understand the broad expanse of salt water, the salmon itself adapts easily to life in the salt. Hatched in small freshwater streams, it swims and drifts on the current downriver to the land's end where its body adapts to the increasing salinity of the water in the mixing zones at river mouths and in tidal estuaries. As the fresh water mingles with the salt water and finally becomes part of the Great Salt, so the salmon mingles with the life of the salt to become both predator and prey in the open sea. It fattens itself in this vast ocean pasture that grows shrimp and herring by the ton. In turn, the salmon is pursued by seals, orcas and mesh nets. As the waters of the land become one with the ocean, so the life of the ocean intertwines and intermixes with the life of the land: salmon born as far inland as Idaho, school in the Bering Sea under angry foam flecks blown off the wave peaks under cold gray skies. The Idaho fish mix with their distant relatives spawned on the Kamchatka Peninsula, also wandering in the salt, growing fat on the ocean's food chain.

Underneath the ocean's surface the salmon of the fresh water feed and grow. On top, the water that once was fresh, that once flowed through salmon's nursery streams in the pine forests of Idaho's Salmon Mountains, evaporates and rises into the air to become clouds. And as the clouds drift toward the continent, so the salmon turn toward home, drawn by the urge to return to their natal waters. The fish of the water and the water of the clouds move with the currents of the sea and the air toward land in the endless cycle that is the hydrological cycle, the life cycle that binds the land, air and water together into one.

And you stand by a stream in the mountains many miles from the salt in the rain and watch a huge, misshapen hen salmon fan its tail creating a redd in the gravel. A buck slides over next to the hen and mixes its milt with the cascade of translucent orange eggs falling slowly and softly into the cobble. The hen swims upstream and washes some gravel over the fertilized eggs. A few days later, grotesque with white fungus, the once sleek silver salmon rolls on its side as the rain peppers the water, its gill plates no longer moving, its life force gone. It drifts onto a downstream gravel bar where an eagle rips into the soft white belly and then flies off into the air, disappearing into the smoky clouds that fuse the sky to the pine-covered earth.

# VIII. THE UNTRUTHFUL ANGLER

AT THE DAWN OF RECORDED TIME THE EPIC POET HOMER noted in *The Iliad* that "The tongue of man is a twisty thing." It is unclear if he had anglers in mind when he made this observation on the human condition, but little has changed in the ensuing three thousand years: truth still is elusive in all matters of human interaction, especially on the angling waters. Why anglers in particular are so often such bald-faced liars always has been a perplexing question. Other sports are given to the occasional stretching of the truth. Golfers, for example, have their "mulligan" whereby they take an extra, unrecorded, stroke.

But anglers toy with the truth in ways incomprehensible to other human endeavors. It is a rare eighteen-inch trout that when confronted with a bona fide tape measure actually measures eighteen inches. It is a rare remembered fishing trip that actually was fishless. And it is rare to ever get a truthful answer to the innocent streamside question: "How's fishing?"

Walton, our guide in so many matters of angling decorum, is of little assistance here as he was a truth stretcher of gargantuan proportions himself. One of his most notorious stretchers is his advice to throw the long cane rod into the water when fighting a large and strong fish, presumably so the drag of the rod will exhaust the fish. Most readers, including Charles Cotton who wrote the fly-fishing section in the fifth edition of *The Compleat Angler*, raise their eybrows at this advice from Father Walton. Yet, I'm told by my barber, a native Midwesterner, that the old-time pike anglers in Minnesota trolled with long cane rods and no reels. When they hooked a good-sized pike they would heave the rod overboard and let the fish tire itself by pulling the cane around, much as a harpooned whale tires by struggling against the floats attached to the harpoon running line. After awhile you retrieve the rod and reach for the landing net. Like so many fishing stories, it all sounds plausible, but...

Truth takes a back seat on any angling journey long before the trip begins. Anticipation of fishing trips is a source of great pleasure to most anglers who spend much less time on the water than they want to given the pressure of jobs, family and other duties. We look forward to the next fishing trip immensely; this anticipation buoys us during our everyday world as we answer phone calls, stare at computer screens, attend meetings, repair garage doors, mow the grass, empty the dishwasher. The prospects for the pending fishing trip are always excellent. On the next trip the water conditions will be just right, the insects will hatch according to schedule and the fish will be feeding aggressively all day long. Hooks will not snag on underwater obstacles or on streamside alder branches. The wind won't blow and the sun won't shine too brightly and put the fish down. There will be a thin gauze of cloud cover. The temperature will be comfortable, not too hot or too cold. And it won't rain.

So far this is only wishful thinking, not lying, but it sets into motion the distorted thinking that accompanies any fishing trip and leads to lying. The prudent businessman would hardly approach a new business venture with such unfailing optimism, but then businessmen are not anglers, or when they are anglers they are off-duty as businessmen. When they hang up the Brooks Brothers suit they leave prudence behind. The fishing vest suggests adventure and enthusiasm, not caution. Anglers are the most optimistic of Homo sapiens. To them the glass is always brim full, not half full and never half empty. Anglers may laugh at the fly-by-night, flimflam salesman to whom the next deal is the best deal, but when they are preparing for a fishing trip it always promises to be the best ever.

This overly optimistic thinking may be the mirror image of the overly negative thinking some of us indulge in on the way to the physician's office: prepare for the worst and you will be pleased with whatever you're told about your physical condition. Perhaps neither attitude is healthy, but it seems part of the human condition that when faced with the unknown we prepare ourselves unrealistically. For anglers, the prospect of poor fishing is rarely considered. It is always going to be a good trip.

This pre-trip distortion of angling prospects is reinforced in a number of ways. Read most any outdoor magazine and you'll find story upon story of great fishing. You'll find pictures of large beautiful fish, deftly landed by successful anglers, ready to be released after the obligatory photo session. You forget that fish this size rarely grace the terminal end of your tackle. But they might one day if you can only glean a few more tips from the experts. Gear advertisements promise success, too, if only you will purchase the newest rod or line or boat or waders. A good number of angling books from Walton's time to our own promise success too if only you will absorb what lies between the covers. Knowledge is powerful medicine on the fishing waters and you can never know too much. You read and read and read and learn more and more and hope you will be a better angler for it. It's all fun, but sometimes I wonder if some of us don't plateau as anglers and reach a point where we don't improve regardless of how much information we absorb. It is probably just me and my limited angling ability, but at times I think I did just as well in my younger days on my home water with an Elk Hair Caddis and Gold Ribbed Hare's Ear than I do now with twenty times the number of flies at my disposal.

Visit a fishing store prior to your trip and with rare exception the talk will be thick with optimism, long on promise. You'll hear about the angling successes of the past few weeks and little of the less-than-successful ventures. This is not entirely the fault of the shop staff. Afterall, they get a skewed view of reality because the guys who get skunked don't come back in the store to brag about it. They slink away into the night, back down the highway, homeward bound. They are searching for excuses to tell their wives and friends. They are convincing themselves of the great time they had just being out in nature.

"It's the act of angling that counts, not the fish tally," they lamely try to persuade themselves as they remember only the feel of slack line on the water.

The guys who return to the shop to brag are the lucky ones who know that the shop help—paid listeners—will hear their stories dutifully, unlike family members who don't care if the fish took a size 14 PMD or a size 18 Parachute Adams.

Outfitters, guides and lodges all take part in the pre-trip ritual of pumping up the client, too. I recall an Alaskan trip when we hired a driftboat guide for the day to take us on the upper Kenai River in search of big rainbows.

"Yes sir, they'll straighten your line!" the guide told us a number of times in a hearty voice about the savage fight of the fish we were soon to catch.

"Big fish, too," the guide told us as we embarked on the river, the chatter of the riffle rising in volume and drowning out his words. Soon we saw hundreds and hundreds of sockeye, already colored bright red, bound for their spawning waters. They were not interested in a fly, or in chasing anything else. I hooked one by floating an egg pattern into its open mouth. No, I didn't feel very good about it, but I had caught a sockeye for the record. (I had a goal—that has since been achieved—of catching all five species of Pacific salmon.) I had my picture taken holding this large fish then I returned it to the water, sending it back to the mass of other fish that looked exactly like it, all swimming upriver, noses into the current, tails undulating slowly in the cold flow. You could stand knee-deep in the water and watch this column of red-colored fish divide as they moved upstream around you. You could look into their eyes and see nothing, no apparent awareness of your presence, no communication, no pupil movement. They were eyes that looked more like the unseeing blankness of a blind man's eyes than those of a seeing creature. I noticed that other anglers along the shore and in boats were catching sockeye and wondered if they somehow had success in getting them to chase a lure or a fly. Later, back in the lower 48, I had my suspicions confirmed when I read an article in a fishing magazine about how to foul-hook migrating sockeye in the mouth.

But we were not seeking sockeye; we were after the big rainbows that we had heard follow the sockeye, feeding on the eggs that don't find their way into the gravel. None of us was having very much luck. I caught a good sea-run Dolly Varden trout, a type of trout I had never caught before. But I was at a loss as to what to do to find the rainbows.

"What other patterns should I be using?" I asked the guide.

"Did ya try an Egg Sucking Leech?" Despite the strange sounding name, this is probably the most common trout pattern in Alaska. Most Alaska streams are not rich in aquatic insect life, but they do have good leech populations that feed on salmon eggs just as the trout do. The pattern looks like a normal dark, long leech with a pink salmon egg shape tied near the eye of the hook. It looks very much like how you imagine a leech would look sucking on a salmon egg.

"Yea, I've tried several. Anything else?" I asked. The silence was long and it became apparent that our guide did not know a great deal about fly patterns. Maybe he offered another lame suggestion; I can't remember. He rowed the boat well, warmed up a beef stew lunch at mid-day and piloted us through some spectacular scenery where moose fed in the river shallows. His talk of line-straightening rainbows ebbed and ceased altogether by mid-afternoon when it became apparent we were not going to catch very many rainbows, and even fewer line-straighteners.

Actually, in my limited experience on Alaskan waters, I suspect that these North Country anglers excel in pre-trip hyperbole. One book I purchased on Alaskan fly patterns included dressings for a number of likely flies along with brief narratives on their application to the northern waters. After describing one particular pattern, the author instructed the reader to cast it out into the current and "HOLD ON," as if the imminent strike by a monster fish would tear the rod from the angler's hands.

Another time, a friend of mine called a fly shop near a well-known Alberta trout river to check on the fishing conditions prior to his pending departure.

"The fishing's great," he was told. "Come on up!" Less than twenty-four hours later he was there standing beside a torrent of brown water, the product of weeks of wet stormy weather.

Perhaps the guy at the shop had not looked out the window in several days.

None of this is meant to denigrate fishing magazines, books, fly shops, guides, lodges or outfitters. It is just that unconsciously we in the angling community are all guilty of the Sin of Unbridled Optimism. While not among the seven deadly sins, this is a sin de minimis, as the lawyers would say, a small, trifling sin. Only anglers (and hunters in their own way, too) are prone to it. This condition appears widespread in the angling community regardless of whether you fish for trout, bass, salmon, stripers, snook or catfish and whether you use a finely crafted graphite fly rod or a closed-bail K-Mart special. We are all afflicted; it is the price we pay for an overly effervescent attitude toward our passion. All this attention to unrealistic pre-trip expectations is important if we are to understand why the angler, ordinarily a straight-laced type of guy, becomes such a liar once he gets on the water and afterwards. He is set up. He sets himself up. He expects too much and he must compensate for this promise that can never be fulfilled.

Now you are on the water. You have read the books, looked at the magazines, talked to the guys at the fly shop and whomever else you were able to reach. Finally, you are on your much-anticipated fishing trip. You are fishing and you'd rather be fishing than doing most anything else in the world. Well, there are a few things you might rather be doing, but not now and not with your present companions who have two days of stubble on their cheeks. You are on top of the world, not a care in the world but whether to fish the slick below the big boulder mid-stream or up against the undercut grassy bank on the other side of the island. The dawn of any fishing trip is a wonderful time, full of promise, full of life as you have hours, maybe days ahead of you to engage in your life's passion. Often you feel a little guilty at first with all this time to focus simply on fishing.

There's no telephone to attend to, no meetings, no kids to be shuttled to games and no grocery shopping to be done. You're as free as you will ever be and soon you start to forget the life of duty and care you left behind.

Reality has a way of settling in on any trip after a few hours, or especially after a few days. You've substituted the reality of your home and office with the reality of the angling waters and even though all is benign initially, after awhile you begin to notice whether or not you are hooking any fish. Sometimes you quickly get into the rhythm of the fishing: the hatches, the casting, wading, mending and you begin hooking fish early on. Other times you have to work at it, hours and hours of casting for each strike. And at other times you never seem to get the knack of it and go all day without success. An animal predator, such as a heron or river otter, would go about its fishing without reflection: fish, eat, sleep, fish. But as a human predator you are saddled with reflection, which can lead to justifications, excuses and lying. You need to make sense of the reality you are immersed in, a reality that has followed your expectations as surely as indigestion follows a night of too much hot sauce on too many enchiladas, rice and beans. When the fishing is great, you are caught up in the moment and you don't give much thought to what you are doing, but when the fishing is slow you attempt to analyze what you might be doing wrong and how you might improve your situation.

But before going any further, let's first look at the fishing log, the only truly accurate account of the trip, an outpost of truth in a land of lies. A genuine fishing log may include some philosophizing, but it will concentrate on recording the facts: weather and water conditions, dates, insect activity, areas where the fish are found, the numbers of fish hooked, what patterns were the most productive, the size and fighting qualities of the fish and so on. This is the simple unvarnished truth that you can refer to later at your bedside. Long ago most of us learned to distrust memory as it often has a way of omitting some events and exaggerating others. As any journalist will tell you, notes taken at the time of the event are the bedrock of reporting. One military historian I recently read said that the truth of the battle varies in direct proportion to the proximity of the note taker to the fighting and the amount of time between the event and its recording on paper.

Yes, you will record the bare facts in your fishing log, but most of us are too prone to pondering to let that be that. Especially if I am fishing poorly, I soon find myself beginning to rationalize about the reality that has confronted me: the water level is too low, the trout are being awfully selective, the water temperature must be too high, the river has been too heavily fished lately, the fish are spooky and so on. Some of this may be true, but much is speculation born out of frustration that great expectations are not being met. If I have landed and released a fish at, say ten inches, and then don't hook another fish for some time, the ten-incher begins to push eleven inches in angling memory. Later twelve.

But real yarn spinning begins when you communicate with others, especially strangers. Seldom is there a truthful answer to the streamside query: "How's fishing?" If it is one of your companions who is doing the asking you probably will reply truthfully. However, some conditions can lead to even good friends lying to one another. For example, if you have been doing terrible and you come across your partner who tells of his great success, it is difficult not to exaggerate your small accomplishments or make up some if need be. Likewise, if the tables are turned you may downplay your success when confronted by your partner's slow fishing. I have long wondered what it is about fishing that can twist the truth even among friends. Part of the reason, it seems, is that when a companion is jubilant about his success you hate to be the dour wet blanket, the droopy-eared Eeyore of *Winnie-the-Pooh*. You don't want your friend feeling sorry for you and you hate to grovel for excuses as to why the fish are avoiding your offerings. Likewise, if you are the one doing well, you hate to rub it in. Maybe you have adroitly discovered the hatch, matched it and are enjoying the fruits of your intelligence. You want to share your information but in a way that is helpful and not boastful.

Ideally, if two anglers are fishing together and are close in fishing abilities, both will experience similar fishing success or lack of success. If everyone is catching a lot of fish there is little problem and if no one is catching fish there is little problem. It's the in-between that can be troublesome. And if the fishing abilities of the companions differ substantially, then the results can vary tremendously. I know of times when one guy has hooked fish well into the double figures while another angler in the same party is skunked. Inequality in all matters of human intercourse breeds problems. In the case of angling it can breed not only lying but the bona fide sin of envy, too. I may be alone on this (I doubt it) but I despise myself for the times I have stood with envy and even a little spite in my heart as a good friend hooks fish after fish while I for some reason go fishless. I should take joy in my friend's success but the green mist of envy has a way of suffocating the fragile human heart.

But we are discussing truth in angling, not angling envy which is a separate topic, and the truth fares especially poorly when it is a stranger and not a friend who asks: "How's fishing?"

"So-so," you respond.

Or you might vary this by saying, "Kinda slow." These responses are the most common answers you hear on the river, regardless of how the fishing has actually been. You don't want to encourage anyone to crowd your waters. Some younger anglers who have done well may actually succumb to bragging about their success, but they will learn. The next time they seek their honey hole it may be occupied.

Some anglers are bothered by actual lying and simply become evasive when asked direct questions. Ask them about the patterns they are using and they will respond with vague generalities.

"Mayfly," they might say with little specificity as to color, size, adult or nymph.

Ask most anglers about actual locations on the river that hold fish and you likely will get an even more vague answer if not downright lies. The hard-bitten angler would sooner share his most intimate secrets than guide a total stranger to his secret spot on the river.

Most anglers enjoy the companionship of one another, strangers or not; we just don't want to get too detailed about the river's secrets that we have uncovered through years of hard work. In fact, a riverside angling conversation between two strangers can be entertaining. On one level they respect one another for the fine avocation they have selected and they have much in common because of that. One the other hand, a fisherman is always fishing, fishing for information, fishing for secrets hard won and rarely revealed. They speak obliquely, talking more about the weather and water conditions at first than actual fishing. They may eventually warm up to one another and discuss fishing. And then, maybe, they will talk about the river that is flowing by in front of their waders. Both will be on guard waiting for an incautious moment when a grain of angling truth might escape.

While the truth may be a fragile vessel when you are on the water, it is shattered altogether afterwards. Memory, reflection and storytelling tend to manipulate the truth of an experience beyond recognition. The recollection of fishing trips is so steeped in lies and exaggerations that even our language has adopted the term "fish story" for broader use. Of course, all this varies with the individual. Some anglers more accurately reflect the truth of their experience than do others. Some are congenital liars. Some are simply the type of people who see the past through rose-colored glasses. In keeping with the optimistic nature of anglers, very few are downright grumpy or pessimistic. You seldom find dour anglers; they are upbeat people who naturally see the bright side of life, especially of their favorite passion. Anglers enjoy the act of fishing, not just the catching of fish, so they can draw sustenance from a fishless trip, though in their heart of hearts they would rather have hooked some fish.

Memory has a way of editing experience, of deleting the long slack periods when you cast out pattern after pattern with no response. Upon reflection, these long hours wither to thin slivers of time and the moments when you had fish on the line stretch out to fill the days. Not long ago I fished my home water for two days with fair to medium results, according to my log. But as the months and years pass I remember less the hours without fish than the minutes when I hooked and lost a real monster rainbow. ("Oh no, here he goes," you say. Be patient. There is a point to this fish story.) When I speak of this trip to fellow anglers it is that ten-to fifteen-minute period that I focus on and not the hours that I know I spent without any fish. My re-telling of the story must leave the impression that it was a great trip because of this editing, this concentration on the moment of excitement. And in a way, in my mind's eye, it was a great trip because of those few minutes.

The episode in question came early on in the trip when we pulled the driftboat onto a mid-river gravel bar and fished around its perimeter. I fished a heavily weighted stonefly nymph on the point and a trailing tiny Serendipity through the swift run on the inside channel. Mid-way through a drift the strike indicator vanished and I felt a hard pull. I set the hook and the fish took off. With the force of the current and the pull of the strong fish the line screamed off the reel. When it got deep into the backing I became worried as the line came off in fits and starts. That part of the Dacron had not seen the light of day in years—maybe ever—and was full of kinks and twists. You don't often get that deep into your trout reel backing.

I realized early on that I would never land the fish; I only hoped for a glimpse of it. I was on the downstream end of the island and could not follow the fish any farther downriver. It is illegal to fish from a boat on this river so I couldn't get in the boat and follow it. I tried backing up slowly, pumping the rod and reeling in a little line. But then the fish would turn and take back what I had retrieved. With less and less backing left I began to increase the pressure on the line and then it went slack. There is no more startling contrast in angling than the difference between the humming of a tight line with a strong fish on and the coils of limp line on the water after a break-off. It's heartbreaking. I reeled in at least one hundred yards of line, maybe more, and to my surprise discovered that the Serendipity had broken off. So much for the adage that large fish eat only large prey.

It has been some time since I hooked and lost this fish, but its image is as clear as ever in my mind. Many other parts of that trip have vanished from my memory, deleted by the internal editor that never sleeps, but that fish and that fight remain. Why is it that the best part of the trip remains vivid? Perhaps it is perfectly natural to remember the exciting and forget the mundane. Whatever the reason, the working of memory is at the root of the angler's losing battle with the truth. He can't help it. Truth is a casualty of memory, an involuntary psychological process we have no control over.

Reflection, a conscious recollection of the past as opposed to the unconscious process of memory, shapes our past trips, too. Here individual anglers differ greatly, too: some get back to work and family duties quickly while others find re-entry into civilian life more difficult. Portions of their minds tend to remain suspended in time: visual and tactile images of the trip remain alive for days and weeks after the trip. This can be a curse or a boon, depending on your point of view. It is as though some of us are like cattle chewing on our cud, ruminating the same meal over and over.

Reflecting on a fishing trip usually produces positive thoughts as it is done against the background of duty and obligation while you are on your way to work, waiting for an appointment or stuck in traffic. It is one of the many pleasures of the angling life that the fishing experience has such sustaining power. It is a mental pleasure to be able to buoy your spirits with the recollection of a recent trip and it naturally leads to speculation on the next trip. Through reflection we come full circle back to the anticipation of the next trip, which is where we began. And, of course, the next trip will be even better than the last one. The next deal is the best deal.

In the end, truth doesn't matter very much in angling psychology. Oh, it does for the really obnoxious liars whom we must tolerate on occasion, the fly-fishing bullies who appear never to have had a bad day on the water, the guys whose gap between word and deed is a chasm. But for the rest of us, the stark naked minute-by-minute reality of each trip is softened by memory and honed by reflection into keen anticipation of the next trip. It's just the way it is, it's another one of the pleasures of the angling life that is ours to enjoy.

# IX. THE ROMANTIC ANGLER

MOST FISHING WIVES, COMMONLY CALLED FISHING widows, would be incredulous at the notion that angling could possibly have anything to do with romance. Usually, angling is seen as the antithesis of romance. The fisherman-husband chases trout in mountain streams all weekend long leaving his wife at home to entertain herself. He spends valuable family financial resources on fishing gear and exotic fishing trips. But regardless of the apparent contradiction in the term—romantic angler—fishing is, at its heart, a romantic endeavor. A man apprenticed to the fishing way of life will over time evolve into a better mate despite his lengthy absences and the unexplained depletion of family funds. Why? Because the fact that he is enamoured with something as unpractical as fishing reveals a man unafraid to act on his feelings. He may not project a traditional romantic image, but the fact that he pursues a passion as intently as he does, a passion that has so little practical value, reveals a guy motivated by the heart. The dedicated angler is a passionate man. He may not always appear passionate, as he needs to maintain a dignified, reasoned exterior to survive in the work-a-day business world where passion is nearly always frowned upon. Logic, reason, the bottom line, is the world of work. Unchaperoned passion will get you nowhere but in trouble in most pursuits, angling excepted. As an elderly stockbroker once told me: emotion drives the market; lack of emotion makes money in the market.

The serious angler may not appear to be a passionate sort of guy, but beneath that floppy, cock-eyed hat and behind those polarized dark-green glasses is a true romantic. Consider the dictionary's definition of romantic: not practical, without a basis in fact, fanciful, quixotic, passionate.

Who better fits these attributes than the angler? He is certainly not a practical guy for what can be practical about trying to catch fish, especially if you release them back into the water after you land them. Club the fish on its head and stuff it in the gunny sack and then maybe you inch closer to the practical, but even most meat anglers are not truly practical. When you add up the cost of your gear, license, gasoline, wear and tear on the car, food, lodging and other expenses the cost per pound of whatever fish you occasionally bring home is far more than you would pay at the fish counter. And the catch-and-release angler is clearly not motivated by practicality, as the moron doesn't even keep what he catches. As a local Indian once said to a fly-fishing friend of mine about the difference between the Indian fishery and the sportfishery: "We don't play with our food."

Another definition of the romantic is that he is without a basis in fact. Again, as we have seen about the elaborate delusional preparations for a fishing trip that lead to angling untruths, the sport of fishing is based more upon conjecture than on fact. Fact, like truth, is a difficult commodity to find on the angling waters. Part of this is the mercurial nature of fishing itself. It may be a fact that the fish are biting at one minute at a certain location, but get there ten minutes later and the bite may be off. Facts on the water are short lived. Off the water, facts hardly exist at all. If we turn to Webster's one more time, it tells us that a fact is a thing that has actually happened or the state of things how they are. Well, it will be a distant day in hell when you will hear a truly factual answer to your question about how the fishing is or what actually happened on a fishing trip. You will hear answers to these and other questions, but they will be not be facts. The answers may contain some factual material, but it will be twisted, embellished and convoluted beyond recognition. If you want facts you don't walk into a fishing store because you won't find any there. You may find dreams, wishful thinking, entertainment, dubious advice and lies, but you will seldom find any facts. The fishing report written on the big chalkboard at the back of the shop masquerades as fact, as though it was filled with algebraic equations or logical syllogisms. But we know that the information on the board, and from lips of the help, will at best be a guess at how the fishing has been the past day or two, and it will be a leap of faith when predictions are made for the next day. At the worst, the information you get in a fishing shop will be bald-faced lies, "shop talk" designed to pump up the customer, get him excited about the angling prospects and purchase more gear.

Another mark of the romantic is that he is fanciful. It would be difficult to find anyone more lost in fantasy than an angler on his way to the river. When he is on the river the actual reality of wading, casting, tying on flies and figuring out how to reach the seam on the outside edge of the backeddie intrudes on his fantasies momentarily. But once off the water, back at camp or back home, the fantasies return of what the next day's fishing will be. Nowadays in sports and in other endeavors we are told to visualize kicking a goal or hitting a baseball or accomplishing whatever task is before us. It is a thin line between visualization and fantasy and most anglers cross back and forth it all the time. The angler's fantasy is not without value. Fantasy keeps the angler alive during the many days and weeks between his trips to the water, just as a different sort of fantasy fuels the lust of lovers who may be separated for days or weeks at a time.

Quixotic is another attribute the dictionary ascribes to the romantic and here too the angler fits the bill. Quixotic refers, of course, to Don Quixote, the impractical, extravagantly chivalrous knight-errant in the satirical romance, *Don Quixote of La Mancha*, by Cervantes published in the early seventeenth century. Don Quixote would make a good dry-fly fisherman. He would be unaffected by the trifling details that might get in the way of his quest for a big brown trout on a size-twenty fly. There he is waving his long greenheart rod in the air, undeterred by the clouds of mosquitoes that have rendered his face a mass of small bumps. Physical pain is nothing to the Knight of the Rueful Figure. The tiny fly has caught on a small branch just under the surface of the water, but Don Quixote mistakes the tight line for a strike and sets the hook with gusto, breaking off the fly and losing his balance. He falls into the water and so on.... All the while Sancho Panza, now his gillie, is mumbling about switching to crank bait and a bobber while searching through his daypack for some more salami and cheese.

Actually, Don Quixote would not be fishing for trout at all, but would be fishing for carp in a muddy creek. In his mind he would be fishing for trout. In his mind he would be in the mountains on a pristine stream angling for bright rainbows, surrounded by green meadows dotted with wildflowers. The carp actually before him in the backwater creek would be twisted by his imagination into rainbows, just as he believes the local buxom village wench is Lady Dulcinea del Toboso.

Don Quixote lives in our imaginations because of the power of his imagination. Today the more clinical among us might call him delusional, but he is who he is because of a vision that turns windmills into giants and a barber's basin into a knight's helmet. Who is to say the fanatical steelheader making his two-hundredth cast of the day—day after fishless day—is any more delusional? What does he expect to happen after flogging the water day after day without a strike? I don't like to recall the number of hours—days—I have spent casting out into the current hoping a steelhead will swing its head to the side, open its mouth and snap at my fly as it drifts across the current. Freight Train, Mack's Canyon, Skykomish Sunrise, Night Dancer, Clown, Purple Peril, Muddler Minnow, Green Butt Skunk—the offerings from the summer steelhead fly-box seem endless and at times are endlessly refused. Isn't the definition of an idiot someone who does the same thing over and over and expects a different result? The dedicated steelheader, or tarpon hunter, or angler of any difficult prey spends day upon day in pursuit of his elusive quarry that he romanticizes in words and thought. He goes out in good weather and in bad, without encouragement, against all odds, against reason, waiting for a hookup that will electrify the man within. He wants that jolt that will make him forget about everything in the world except a large, leaping fish on the end of a long line. The fight will still time, hush the river and focus his concentration as nothing else can. In the end he will drag the fish into the shallows and marvel at its brilliant silver sides tinged pink and violet along the lateral line. He will look into the dumb, unresponsive eyes of his catch and realize the limits of communication with the natural world. If it is a hatchery fish he may break its neck and later feed on its flesh. If it is a wild fish he will treat it gently, cradle it in his hands while it regains its strength. He will watch its gill plates expand and contract more quickly and then he'll feel a ripple in its sleek body as it regains its vigor and slips away from him, back into the flow. The angler's quest may not be encumbered with giants and dragons but it is as quixotic of an adventure as you could find in our time.

Finally, the romantic is defined as one who is passionate, and the dedicated angler comes to mind again. What but passion fuels his ability to stand in hip-deep water all day long casting through a cold rain against a stiff wind, his hands so numb he hopes his tackle will not break off because he knows he won't be able hold a strand of monofilament in his thick fingers and tie on another hook. To be passionate about something is a wonderful thing, a spontaneous feeling that can't be willed. When you are passionate about something you don't have to be motivated by money or praise. It is not a chore; it is something you care deeply about and want to do.

Young people usually have passion in ample amounts but as we age many of us lose the capacity to be passionate. The wear and tear of forty-hour workweeks year after year, adult responsibilities, adult sorrows, all eat away at whatever passions we once had. You say you don't have time for passion, that you're too busy, too overly committed and so on. And passion often succumbs to ambition and that leads to longer and longer work hours and a debilitating single-mindedness. After a while you slowly lose interest in those things that used to excite you: maybe it was music or gardening or basketball or swimming in a cold mountain stream on a hot August afternoon. Your spirit blood drains from your system and you move around like a robot, efficiently functional in all matters, but lifeless, vapid. It is a vicious circle as all work and no play does indeed make Jack a dull boy, so you lose even more of your capacity for passion. You become a good provider, a good corporate citizen, a good consumer and a shell of a human without spark, without soul.

The dedicated angler does not walk this path. His passion for fishing keeps his life in balance. You don't have to worry about him working overtime, he barely has time to work regular hours. If he didn't have to work full time to survive, he would work part time. He doesn't live to work; he works to live.

There's the story of the Canadian backcounty Indian who worked a three-day week at a remote sawmill.

"How come you only work three days a week?" a fellow worker asked the Indian.

"Because I couldn't get by on two," the Indian answered, something the dedicated angler understands completely. If the angler could get by working three days of week, he probably would, too.

Passion in the angler does not wither away as it does in so many others. The angler acts on his passion on a regular basis. It motivates him, invigorates him, keeps him in touch with his emotional self. To be passionate about something is a deeply human trait that springs from within. You fiddle with it at your risk. Extinguish passion and your eyes lose their sparkle, your voice flattens. There's no guaranteed way to rekindle passion once it's gone. It is not like rebuilding a house that has burned down. Like falling in love, you either are passionate about something or you are not. You can't make two people fall in love, nor can you force a passion for angling or any other endeavor.

Passionate, quixotic, fanciful, without fact, unpractical—all these attributes of the romantic are found in the angler in ample proportions. The angler is not obvious about his romantic nature; maybe he is even a little self-conscious about it. Maybe he doesn't even recognize it. He may think he is a hard-boiled, rod and reel, "Eat, Sleep and Go Fishing" sort of guy. He is so immersed in his passion, so lost in his quixotic quest for more fish and larger fish that he can't see the romance in it. But the angler's quest is romantic. It is subtle, like the slow, slack line dry-fly drift downstream into the feeding lane of a rising fish.

Because angling is ultimately a romantic endeavor, it nurtures that side of you that is often buried by reason and duty. It puts you in touch with the natural world, a world with less attitude and more nuance. If you are going to be successful as an angler you learn to be open to changing conditions whether it is changes in the weather, hatches or river levels. You slow down and learn to listen to the river, to read its complex currents, to map its unseen rocky bottom in your head. You can come to the river and not take the time to observe and listen, but you will not catch as many fish, nor will you take away much at the end of the day other than some fish flesh, perhaps. Rivers have a way of flowing through you if you let them, taking away the tension you bring from your man-made life and replacing it with a more natural rhythm. After spending time on the water you are more attuned to the natural flow of life, and this includes romance, for what is more natural than love? There is little logic to romance. You are in love or you aren't. You can't will it or plan it. Today our lives are too often overplanned. Appointment books and calendars are filled months in advance. Vacations—to get away from it all—are planned months ahead, often with the hours of each day planned out too. Go to a popular tourist destination without advance tickets to the sights and you're in trouble. We plan career paths, investment strategies and retirement accounts. But you can't plan whom you will fall in love with, what disputes may arise or how long your love will last. So it goes on the angling waters. You can make the best plans, bring all the right gear, be prepared for all types of weather and so forth. But you can't plan the fishing. The fish may be on the bite and they may not be.

There may be a reason why they are not biting, but most often you will not have the slightest idea why the bite is off or on. You will use a combination of logic and intuition to solve the puzzle, but in the end it may come down to luck.

Anglers also are sensitive guys because fishing is accompanied by failure as often as it is by success. If you fish enough you will have been skunked a number of times and nothing fosters sensitivity to your own failings and to others' needs more than the humility of defeat. An angler who is always successful would be unbearable. Defeat humanizes you. Look at the sports' stars. When they win a game they seem larger than life. They have accomplished difficult athletic feats and made it seem easy. They raise their arms and shout with victory. They seem far removed from our everyday lives. By contrast, when a star suffers defeat he is quiet at the end of the game. His hands are at his sides, not up in the air giving the victory sign. Then we identify with him; he seems human, like us. Of course, none of us want to lose all the time on the basketball court or on the river, but the occasional defeat, as happens all too often in fishing, makes you a fuller person.

Sometimes I consider myself an expert on failure, angling failure that is, and while it may have made me a more empathic person it also has driven me nuts. For example, I have now fished Henry's Lake twice without a strike. For the uninitiated, Henry's Lake is located on the Idaho-Montana border, the source of the famed Henry's Fork of the Snake. It is considered one of the best fly-fishing lakes in the country with anglers traveling from around the world to fish its waters. You can fish it from a boat or float tube and you will likely use a leech imitation or a damselfly nymph or some other pattern. The lake is in a bowl-shaped valley with the mountains around you startling in their beauty and massiveness. Snow-patched granite sawteeth define the horizon line against a brilliant blue sky that seems crisper and bluer than usual because you are at such a high altitude. It is always a fascination in the natural world how the color of the sky changes, how it is colored at all. The astronauts and high-altitude jet pilots talk of the sky darkening as you climb up through the stratosphere, as you leave behind the cushioning layer of life giving gases that envelope our world of water and rock. At the edge of the atmosphere they say the sky is a midnight blue, deep, rich and fading into the blackness of space.

Airborne, but closer to the waters of the lake than the bright blue sky, fly large white pelicans, diving into the water from time to time to scoop up fish in their jumbo-sized beaks. A thicket of fishing boats cluster against the inlet edge of the lake, anglers casting into the thick glow of the early morning light. We cast out, too, letting our lines sink to bottom before beginning the retrieve. One of us is in the bow and the other in the stern and we cover the water in all directions. As the day brightens the early morning haze and mist evaporates, leaving behind air that is stunningly clear and clean, like the glass pane of a window that you have just cleaned with a soft, dry squeaky cloth. The sun rises higher in the sky and you pull off your wool sweater that was comfortable at dawn and reach for the sunscreen.

You think of what you heard and read about the lake and expect it to be thick with large fish, ready to strike. But on my two mornings on the lake, some four years apart in time, this has not been the case. The rainbow-cutthroat hybrids that populate the lake grow to a large size but don't easily come to a fly, at least to the fly on the end of my tippet. My companion on both trips had two fish each time take his fly, but the fish shunned my offerings. To date, I am fishless at Henry's Lake. I remain fishless at some other lakes, too, but they are not lakes of any renown, so the skunked stigma is not as hardfelt. I suspect from watching the unmoving rods of other nearby anglers, that I was not alone in my lack of luck on those two days, but you would never know this by consulting the list of top fly-fishing lakes.

One of the mountain lakes where I once had some excellent fishing is probably not on any list. I believe it was called Twin Lakes in northeastern Washington state, not the large Twin Lakes Resort on the Colville Indian reservation, but a much smaller pair of lakes. We did not see another camping party and we never saw another angler. We didn't see any sunbathers or swimmers either, as the weedy shoreline was not conducive to the beach scene. In mid-day when it was hot and the kids wanted to swim we would row the rubber raft out into the deeper water and use it as a swimming platform. It worked fine until the kids discovered a few small leeches attached to their skin.

"Don't worry about it," I told them. "They're harmless, part of the food chain. All lakes have 'em. Just brush 'em off."

Not surprisingly, my words were of little comfort, no matter that they were true. By my standards these leeches were a good sign, a sign of abundant trout food and a minor inconvenience when swimming. To others, the small leeches were foot-long tropical bloodsuckers.

In the early evening we would row the raft around the perimeter of the lake and every time we passed a certain rocky shoreline on one side of the lake we would get strikes. We didn't hook them all, not even most. But we had a lot of strikes and that was the key. We were trolling a Flatfish on a spinning rod and a leech (of course) on a fly rod. Despite our hooking ineptness we had quite a few fish on the line, even a few double hookups. We kept several of these medium-sized cutthroats for the pan as there appeared to be so many in the lake and the regulations allowed for killing a number of fish a day. Their flesh was dark pink, unusually dark for such small fish, and rich tasting. Their eyes deadened and hollowed as they cooked in the hot oil of the cast-iron frying pan. Their tails curled and their flour-starched backs stiffened, then blistered. You wedged your fork in along the tiny backbone and scraped off one half of the flesh and crisp skin, and then you peeled away the backbone from the other half of the fish that still lay before you. I can't recall if we had the foresight to have a fresh lemon in the food box, but I hope we did. The aroma of frying fish filled the morning air and I was glad we were not in grizzly country. I was glad we were where we were, at a good camp on a good lake in good country. And it was good to be eating of the local waters, closing the last links of the food chain that included the leeches, trout, and now us.

It is good too to be successful fishing now and again so that getting skunked is not bothersome. If you have fished long enough you don't expect to always catch fish, and your eyes narrow when talking to other anglers who never seem to have had a bad day on the water. If you are always successful, on all waters and in all days, my guess is that you have an inaccurate memory or that you are a liar. The honest angler eats his humble pie now and again. It may not taste good, but like some medicines, it's good for you. If you always caught a lot of fish, big beautiful fish, you would be a swaggering, intolerable boor not only on the angling waters but at home, too. The honest angler has been shown his station in life and knows his limits. He is a sensitive guy, a humble guy, a guy better suited to romance than an overly confident braggart who has always had things go his way.

Master Walton's characters also are not without their romantic moments. At the end of the fishing day, before returning to the country inn for supper, they seek out a local milkmaid who will sing them a romantic ballad. They trade part of their day's catch for the pleasure of a ballad that begins:

Come, live with me, and be my love,
And we will all the pleasure prove
That valleys, groves, or hills, or field,
Or woods and steepy mountains yield.

The milkmaid's mother answers with a companion song, the lyrics more melancholy reflecting her years and cares. The milkmaid sings a final song and the anglers, now full of romantic song, move on to the inn for food and drink.

Singing milkmaids are more difficult to locate nowadays, but every day anglers on their way home from the fishing waters turn on the car radio and listen to song. Not much as changed over the years and a great deal has changed. We use graphite rods instead of wooden ones. We use high-tech lines of man-made compounds instead of braided horse hair. And we use monofilament leaders rather than catgut. Yet the desire to fish, the angling passion, still springs from the heart as it always has. It is in the end a romantic notion undeterred by logic, unpractical and totally unnecessary in our post-industrial economy.

# X.  The Aging Angler

LIKE FINE WINES, ANGLERS AGE WELL, USUALLY IMPROVING with the years. Whether we begin fishing as children or not until middle age we will change our fishing methods, interests and abilities as time moves on. Most of us will not fish the same way at seventy-five years old as we did at twenty-five. Physically and philosophically we will approach the waters with a different step. We will look for a different sort of sustenance from the rivers of our youth compared to the rivers of old age.

The youthful angler does not think of these things, as does the older angler, for he has little perspective on the matter. After all, the old angler has had the experience of having been young while the young angler has never been old. To the young angler, fishing and everything else in life is new and he or she goes at it with the directness of youth untempered by time. To be young and on a good piece of water casting worms or Rooster Tail spinners or Pale Morning Duns into the flow is a wonderful bedrock of experience. Unencumbered by time you are immersed in the moment, free of memories of other trips, other fish, other companions, other days, free of the knowledge that your days are numbered, that there is no forever, that time may be without end but your time is not. Your youthful energy is pinpointed on the red and white bobber floating just beyond the weed bed in the bass pond, or on the mechanical whirling sound of the spinning reel's gears as you retrieve a Dardevle around the edge of that submerged log.

Young anglers also are immersed in the moment because it takes their full concentration to get things right. You haven't tied a thousand cinch knots when you are nine years old; you need to think about it. You haven't felt the nibble of a perch or rainbow trout a hundred times. You don't know exactly when to set the hook. The first few fish, good fish, on the line are an experience that stays with you for a long time. For most of us, youth is when we first communicate with the life of the water, the two-way conversation that we will seek the remainder of our days. We all have different childhood fishing memories: mine center on summer days on the river in search of perch and smallmouth with worms and spinners and crayfish. And you remember the total angling experience, not just the hooking of the fish. I can still feel the rush of water on my legs as I wade upstream in shallow water wearing muddy Converse tennis shoes, overturn a rock and feel for crawdads in the declivity. You couldn't see them as the upturning of the rock muddied the water, but you could sure feel them when they grabbed onto one of your fingers with their claws.

I've watched my children shout with joy at hooking small trout, sensing in their thrill the excitement that fish on the line bring to us. This magic of the throbbing rod, running line, leaping fish works on us much the same at eight years old or eighty. True, the childhood thrill of a hooked fish dims and vanishes as adulthood nears for many people, but for those of us who are life-long angling addicts, it never dies. The childhood wonder and unbridled excitement of fish on the line lives in the fisherman and keeps him young. The gray-whiskered angler tying on another fly with dimming eyesight and gnarled fingers doesn't look the picture of youth, but in his heart is a child's delight in the quest, the thrill of pursuit.

In a way, we anglers never really grow up. We never become totally immersed in the stuff of adulthood: careers, mortgages, parental responsibilities, financial planning and so forth. Oh, we take on these responsibilities and certain other adult affectations in order to survive, but we are more than the sum of these parts. Lurking beneath the button-down façade is the fun-loving angler of youth waiting to concentrate his energies on something as unpractical as hooking a fish.

"A fish, for God's sake," many non-anglers say. "How can a grown man with a career and family responsibilities devote so much attention to fishing?"

It is one of the wonders of the angling life that despite the burdens and responsibilities of adult matters, the temptation of the fishing waters burns ever brightly. Angling keeps you in touch with a youthful part of yourself that otherwise might wither away. It is not that you fish the same way as an adult as you would as a child. Hardly. Your angling methods are far more complex, and it is not clear if this is for good or bad. But it is the joy and excitement of the undertaking that remain constant from youth to old age.

Anglers don't become grumps as they age. They may become "old-timers", but not grumps. They may become ornery at times, but not grumps. True grumps—and there are many in the adult population—have lost the capacity to experience spontaneous joy. True grumps focus on the practical: the rest is "humbug"—Ebenezer Scrooge was not a fisherman. If you are a devoted angler you cannot be a grump because the focus of your life is on the impractical. Who needs to fish anymore for practical reasons? To help fill the family larder? Rarely nowadays. Most of us don't even eat what we catch anymore now that catch-and-release fishing is so widely practiced. We fish for fun. And fun, true unmediated spontaneous fun, is the province of childhood. How much real fun you have in your life depends on how much of a child you still are. Too many adults have driven out the child within and no longer know how to have fun. Fishing is fun. No matter how serious some in the angling community get about fishing—and many get way too serious—people fish because it is fun. It can be more than that too, a near transcendental experience for some, but at its roots it is fun. Children understand this and that's why they instinctively enjoy fishing.

For young anglers, fishing means catching fish and they have little patience for the slack hours when the bite is off. They are on the water to catch fish, not to get away from it all or relax or enjoy the natural world. They have little tolerance for long hours of fruitless casting. They make good crappie anglers, poor steelheaders. Attention to the other moments of the angling experience begins weaving its way into the angler's consciousness after he leaves childhood. This happens slowly and almost imperceptibly, but by your 30s you begin to become aware that there is more to fishing than catching fish. Sure you still want to catch fish—a lot of them and large ones at that—but you begin taking pleasure from a day on the water when the river conversation has been largely one-way. This is a different type of angling pleasure than the fun of the strike and the fun of the fight. That is what drew us to fishing as children, but we discover there is more to it than that. You still desire to hook fish and land them, but the childhood world of black and white is slowly coloring. Before, as a child, the time between strikes was without merit. As the angler ages he begins to appreciate this negative space, as the artists call it. You begin to notice that you have enjoyed time on the water when not much was happening at the end of your line.

Not long ago on one of many fishless winter steelhead trips, I stood alongside a long, broad drift casting into the flow, watching my two companions downriver of me casting too, waiting, waiting, waiting. An unusually warm and bright late-winter's day it was and the late-afternoon sun gave the water chop a bright copper glow. It was a river of golden light sliced by heavy lines searching for a fix, a river of transitory lighting that only can be experienced by the angler who sees the ever-changing play of light on the water in all seasons and in all weathers. I lowered the brim of my hat and adjusted my sunglasses to withstand the golden glare. If I was a photographer, I would take a shot of this favorite run at ten-minute intervals throughout the day to record the changing light and piece the prints together in a long montage. But I'm not a photographer so the bright golden flow burned its image into my memory and days later when at the office or behind the wheel in traffic or in bed at night I can see in my mind's eye the glitter of the riffle and I can hear the chatter of the chop at the top of the run and the silence of the deep pool below. You begin to notice these and other things about the waters you fish as you age, and you take these images and memories home with you.

Much has been written about the stages of the angler's life from catching the most fish to the biggest fish to the most challenging fish and so forth. And much of this is true, for most seasoned anglers outgrow the gunny sack mentality somewhere along the way. This progression in angling, however, also involves other changes too such as employing new methods, new strategies, fishing new waters and for new types of fish. Angling is a journey not a destination. Even if we fish the same water year after year we bring different tactics to it season in and season out. We create different fly patterns, fish them in new ways, seek out runs that we once overlooked but that now hold fish. Likewise, you abandon old runs that used to hold fish but have been altered beyond recognition by winter floods, debris or slides. Trying new methods, adjusting to changing conditions, experimenting, traveling to new waters is what keeps the aging angler young. While he may fish decade upon decade, he is never doing the same thing from one trip to the next. Every trip is different. Each time you confront different conditions and employ different methods to hook fish.

As Walton said: "For Angling may be said to be so like the Mathematics that it can never be fully learned."

Another mark of the aging angler is that he stretches out his fishing pleasure by fishing less. This is all in the divine scheme of life as the older angler cannot physically wade up and down the river from morning to night in search of fish. His legs won't stand for it and neither will his back, heart or other parts of the deteriorating physical plant. But that's all right. He doesn't want to rush about, he enjoys sitting on the bank watching the water, taking a nap, not hurrying as a youngster hurries from run to run to cover as much water as daylight allows. And the older fisherman probably is the better angler for it. In his more relaxed state he notices fish winks on the bottom, subtle rises mid-stream, oviposting stoneflies in the late afternoon, slicks, pockets and foam lines that he wouldn't see if he was fishing more hurriedly.

Not long ago I was on a backpack with some companions of late middle age and we talked of former hikes in more youthful days—longer in duration, more miles per day, steeper, rougher, tougher.

"Well," Marty said with a pause as we rested on a shale scree slope along the crest of the Cascade Mountains. We were watching a herd of mountain goats graze on the cliffs below us. The warm, thin, high-altitude air smelled fresh and cool because of an updraft moving across the mushy mid-day surface of a small glacier nearby. "I could still do it, but I just don't want to," he said.

And so it goes with the aging angler: he probably could push harder, get a few more casts in per day, but he doesn't see the need. His enjoyment is not confined to catching more and more fish. There is something satisfying about just being on good angling water. One angling friend now tells me he casts much less when on a good stretch of water than in years past. He is content being there and observing. He notices much more about the river, the holding water, the feeding lanes and the hatches as he stands nearly motionless for long periods of time. This is not easy to do for many of us; it is a skill acquired through age and patience. It is always tempting to cast and cast and cast and change fly after fly in the hope of uncovering the secret of the angling moment. But you learn that sometimes these secrets can be revealed by attentive inaction rather than action. It's the unusual youthful angler who can calmly face a feeding frenzy and analyze the hatch. Even some of us who are no longer young find this difficult to do.

The youthful angler usually wants to push just a little harder, cover more water per minute, hook more fish. He is more destination oriented and does not enjoy each step of the journey as much as does the older angler. This youthful trait is evident in pursuits other than fishing, too, such as hiking. The teenage hiker is usually in a big hurry to get to the destination. During my scoutmaster days I remember one arduous five-day backpack in the high Cascades. In addition to mosquitoes and steep terrain we also had to contend with rain and wet snow in the middle of August. On the fourth day our trail had become a faint path on a high-elevation ridge. There was scenery on all sides that would have been breathtaking had the fog and clouds lifted off the deck. At times the trail would go through the timber and it would be easy to follow. Then it would break out into a large alpine meadow and braid like a river flowing into a delta. The area was well used by elk and most of the braids were elk paths that looked exactly like a hiker's trail. We spread out and tried to find the trail with more human tracks than elk tracks. In other places, the trail vanished on steep rocky ridges where bootprints left no marks on the hard rock. We hiked up higher and higher in altitude, above the small, twisted firs, still in the mist, our bodies and our spirits dampened by the clouds that seemed tethered to the ground. Then we dropped down the other side of the ridge, back into the timber. Less than an hour later we were climbing back out of the timber into open country again, up some switchbacks to the saddle of a bony ridge. I was exhausted when we reached the crest and I took off my pack and sat down to rest.

"Why are we stopping here?" asked one of the boys. I looked at him through glasses that were streaked with sweat. I could feel my heart pounding and was short of breath. My shoulders felt as though a refrigerator had been strapped to my back all day. By contrast, most of the boys seemed to need only a drink from their water bottles. Then they were ready to descend the ridge, in a hurry to get to a camp spot for the night, in a hurry to hike as many miles possible that day in order to shorten the hike on the final day. They were focused on getting to the trailhead, on getting into the cars and stopping at the first fast-food restaurant we could find along the highway. I was tired and in no hurry to move, plus we had worked hard to get this deep into the wilderness and I wanted to enjoy our time here.

"Why are we stopping here?" I could still hear the youthful question.

"Because you're fifteen and I'm almost fifty. That's why," I answered.

It is ironic, of course, that the aging hiker or angler is the one not in a rush as he is the one with less time left on the Big Clock. Some of us have already landed our last fish; we just don't know it. Yet it is the aging angler who takes the time to enjoy the moment at hand because he better understands the experience, the meaning of his brief time on the timeless water. Time may be without measure but not our time which is measured hour by hour, day by day. The aging angler values his time on the water, savors it more than he did in his youth, because he knows how little of it there is left. I imagine that the days on the water in late old age are appreciated in a way unfathomable to me now.

The aging angler enjoys more thoroughly the many ancillary elements of fishing: the setting up of the fishing camp, a slow cold beer before dinner, cooking a fine meal on the Coleman stove, an evening campfire. He doesn't have to be on the water every minute to enjoy the trip, and he finds pleasure in watching his companions discover the joys of the water. Fewer are the hurried trips with long early morning drives to the water, a full day of fishing and a long late-night drive home. More are the overnight trips where the hours on the water far outnumber the hours in the car. The mark of a good trip is when you don't have to re-case your rod at the end of the day.

As anglers we are fortunate that we can enjoy our passion into ripe old age, unlike some other endeavors that require the strength and agility of youth. Already, before three score years are gone, I know my days as a mountain climber and a chukar hunter are numbered. Long ago various skeletal ailments brought to an end my days as a downhill skier and a basketball player. But fishing can be done with the vigor of youth and the discomforts of old age, too. Your knees weaken sooner when wading the swift waters, and in the twilight you have trouble tying on the size 22 emerging midge pupa. But usually you can accommodate for this slippage in a variety of ways, and hopefully you balance your declining physical abilities with increased angling wisdom. You know more than you think you do as an older angler, but you often don't realize it until a less experienced companion begins asking questions. Then you find yourself pouring forth a river of knowledge that you simply had taken for granted but that is all new information to your neophyte friend.

And it is a testament to the ever optimistic spirit of anglers—those to whom the glass is always half full—that despite the growing physical limits of old age that we can always wring great pleasure from our pursuit of fish. I have a copy of a letter that I found in a private fishing library from the late Ted Trueblood to a fellow outdoor writer, Lee Richardson, written Dec. 6, 1978. In the letter the aging Trueblood, a fine and quiet voice in outdoor literature for many decades, complains of a mountain of ailments that have forced "a rather poor year sportwise:" a gimp leg, the discovery of prostate cancer and resulting radiation therapy, and most recently the onset of "the God damned arthritis" in both knees.

"Still, by taking it easy I've managed quite a bit of hunting for grouse, chukars, and quail," Trueblood writes. "And I've really had some splendid fishing—for little, wild trout in the high country in late August and early September and later good dry-fly fishing for rainbows running from 12 inches to 2 and 1/2 pounds in the South Fork of the Boise, which is two hours from home. This stream is making a great comeback with a limit of three fish over 12 inches and single, barbless hooks required. Next year is going to be better!"

Next year? From a man laid low by a combination of ailments that would send others to the rest home, this is a testament to the indomitable angling spirit. For the angler, there is
always the next season, the next riffle around the next bend in
the river, the next flutter of mayflies against the purple pink
horizon of a darkening sky, the next strike of a strong trout,
and the next fight as the line knifes through the deep water and
the spooling reel screams loud under the streamside alders. The
angling spirit is a life force nonpareil, ever able to sustain us in
our days from youth to old age.

# XI. The Fireside Angler

FOR MOST ANGLERS, WINTER IS DOWN TIME. YOU MAY GO OUT a few times to test the frigid waters, but even the most dedicated winter steelheader must move hearth side during long periods of foul weather when the rivers muddy and the channels move knee-deep into the streamside alders. The energetic, well-organized angler utilizes this slack time to tie flies for the approaching seasons, lubricate reels, build another rod, clean fly lines and inventory gear. But the rest of us procrastinating, lazy anglers find this a grand time to simply relax in the easy chair in front of a warm fire and ruminate about our chosen passion.

Non-anglers in the household are always surprised about how much time and energy you can devote to fishing when you are not fishing. They don't understand, of course, the aura that surrounds the reflective angler in his easy chair. A few decades ago this ambience came in part from the physical presence of pipe smoke as the angler puffed away on a fine Cavendish blend while in front of the fire. Today, the pipe or cigar—if we imbibe at all—is most likely limited to the times when we are on the water, or perhaps it is allowed on the deck or in the garage, but rarely is it a fixture in the house.

Deprived of his traditional pipe, the fireside angler will want a beverage of some sort to help him at his fireside chores: it may be a cup of strong Earl Grey tea that sits by his armchair. Or maybe it is a cup of rich, dark roasted coffee, or a soft drink, or a shot of bourbon splashed over an ice cube. Or maybe your winter beverage is a dark ale, such as a Porter, less sweet than the traditional English stout but still with a great caramelized molasses flavor tempered by the bitter hops. The best taste is the first one, after you allow a thick head to build in the mug and then skim off the creamy blonde foam. Flecks cling to your moustache and the creamy froth is thick with the nostalgia of dark English nights in stone inns under fierce North Sea skies.

Whatever your drink, you have it armside, next to the easy chair and on the other side of the chair is an end table with a pile of printed material that could occupy you long into the night. Many nights. To some this material may seem like a helter-skelter pile of books, magazines, maps and catalogs. To you it is an opening into another world that allows you to transport yourself from your chair to the banks of a summer trout stream alive with mayfly hatches and twenty-inch fish crowding the feeding lanes. If you are an aging male angler, you may remember that years ago your tableside pile might have included some more licentious material. With more years on your resume, bifocals resting on your nose and a less frequent need to satisfy the spawning impulse, your leering is confined now more to photos of well-shaped trout than well-shaped women. If you are a younger angler and your pile of printed matter does contain a few such magazines, it's all right: the pondering angler casts a wide net. Enjoy your youth and enjoy your appetites.

If the fireside angler was more motivated by logic than passion he would systematically catalog articles from his various magazines for future use. Probably some anglers do maintain filing systems with clippings on various fly patterns, where to fish on different rivers, ways to improve your dry presentations, nymph-fishing pointers and so on. But most of us are not that organized. We should be, and we probably would catch more fish if we were more organized, but we're anglers not accountants. And if we are accountants, we are off duty now and not organized. We are here to relax and over a period of weeks and months we let this material sink into our fishing selves. As fly-anglers we should relax more. In some ways, fly fishing has become too studied and too refined. Those who really know the hatches hour by hour, month by month, how to imitate them, how to present them and so forth probably catch more fish, but then fishing is about more than catching fish.

In addition to the magazines on the end table there will be several books that you have taken from your library or recently purchased. Winter is a great time not only to read some new titles, but re-read some of the classics, or portions of them, to put you in touch with the bedrock of your angling self. When I feel in a mood for five-dollar words, I call these books my philosophical antecedents. They ground me to who I am, why I'm here and what is important in life.

Of course, the seminal writing in all this literature is Master Walton who wrote during the heady days of the maturing

English language, not long after Shakespeare. There appears to be no evidence that Walton and Shakespeare knew one another even though they were only a generation apart: Walton was in his early 20s when Shakespeare died in 1616 at the age of 52. Technologically our world is far different today than in Walton's merry old England, but his approach to angling as the contemplative man's pursuit remains as true as ever because our basic human characteristics have not changed. We make it through these long winter months because we can contemplate, and in the depths of memory and recollection you can almost feel the tug of a thin-water take by that large rainbow you never were able to land two summers ago. We contemplate the coming seasons and plan our ventures knowing that much of the joy of each trip is in the anticipation and the remembering; the time spent on the water is only the kernel of the trip. We contemplate today no differently than Walton did in his time. We enjoy stalking fish on a scenic stream in the same way that he did. We thrill at the take and the fight whether the bent rod is made of wood or graphite. We toast the end of the fishing day with a bottle of beer just as he and his companions hoisted a flagon of ale at a county inn. We slip a compact disk into the car stereo on the drive home from the water and listen to music just as he and his companions listened to the milkmaid's song on their way back to the inn in the evening. We are separated from Walton and others in the distant past by time but not by our character which has altered little over the centuries.

As in Walton's time, today's anglers, especially fly-anglers, love the written word. It is difficult to imagine a sport, if you can call angling a sport, with as well developed a literature as angling. Since Walton's time thousands of books have been published on angling and magazine articles by the tens of thousands have been published. To have a vibrant literature requires writers and readers and apparently in the angling community we have an ample supply of both. One outdoor magazine editor I talked with not long ago commented on the large number of submissions of stories on fly fishing. It is as though the fly rod and reel manufacturers issued a word processor upon each new sale, he said. Another commentator on the subject suggested, in a more mean spirited vein, that there were simply too many angling books being published today, and that angling writers should be paid not to write books, just as the federal government pays farmers not to grow crops.

Angling literature is a diverse lot. Most commonly we divide it into two broad categories: the practical and the philosophical. Like most taxonomy applied to human endeavors, there are many blurry areas where the two categories overlap. Still, for the purposes of the fireside angler, the stack of books at his side likely has representatives from both camps. And depending on his mood, the fireside angler will select one or the other. Sometimes you get both the practical and philosophical in one, as Walton gave to his seventeenth-century readers. Most modern-day readers gloss over the bulk of his book that offers practical advice on the habits of various fishes and advice on how to catch them. But much of this practical advice is very good: he gives detailed instructions on how to cure certain baits, the life cycle of fishes, how to rig tackle and so forth. If you were a would-be angler in England in the late 1600s you would be well served by Walton's practical instruction. And if you were a would-be fly-angler, you would be equally well served by the fifth edition of the book that includes Charles Cotton's instructions on fly fishing.

But *The Compleat Angler* has remained in print so many centuries not because of this practical advice. If that were all, it would be a curiosity piece read by only a few angling bibliophiles devoted to the evolution of sport fishing. Most modern readers skim much of the passages on carp and eels and how to bait a minnow. What gets close attention are the on-target observations about how to live a contented life, a subject as relevant today as in Walton's time. In a style that is at once playful and didactic, Walton gives us a recipe for a fulfilling life that far surpasses what we hear nowadays from dozens of self-help books. A deeply religious man, he tells us to be content with what God has allotted us and not to toil for what you don't need. He instructs us not to ignore money, but at the same time not to expect that money alone will bring happiness for "there be as many miseries beyond riches as on this side of them." Praise God for good health, he says, for it is a blessing that money cannot buy. And he tells us to maintain a good conscience. "He that loses his conscience has nothing left that is worth keeping," Walton quotes from his French contemporary Nicholas Caussin.

Such nuggets of wisdom in a book on fishing set a high standard for later angling writers. Today you would be hard pressed to find a fishing book with as much practical advice as is included in *The Compleat Angler* that also includes such insightful philosophy as well. Angling literature seems more bifurcated today into the practical and non-practical categories. And with one or two exceptions, it is difficult to imagine Walton's work appearing in today's outdoor magazines, intent as they are on the how-to and where-to. You would gather from much of the writing on fishing nowadays that we anglers, especially fly-anglers, are a very serious bunch indeed—tightly focused on hooking as many large fish as possible in a day. There would be little room today for a writer such as Walton who loved angling because it resolved the eternal tension between living an active life or a contemplative one. "Both these meet together, and do most properly belong to the most honest, ingenuous, quiet, and harmless art of Angling," he said.

Or, as Walton says in "The Angler's Song:"

> Of recreation there is none
> So free as Fishing is alone;
> As other pastimes do no less
> Than mind and body both possess:
> My hand alone my work can do,
> So I can fish and study too.

Like Shakespeare's imposing legacy to subsequent dramatists, so Walton created an enduring monument of angling literature that even to write of him is to hold a candle to the sun, as the Scottish writer Andrew Lang said in his preface to an 1896 edition of *The Compleat Angler*. Still, we must write of him and speak of him from generation to generation in order to keep his spirit alive. And each age must create writers who explore the angling experience in their own time and in their own style for that is the nature of literature. Otherwise, we'd have settled in with a few classics and muted our own voices a long time ago.

A winter's reading for the fireside angler will entail not only a look again at his dog-eared copy of Walton, but at many other writers, too. The mix of writing will depend on the angler: the more practical minded among us will select books that will help him tie better flies, help him identify what insects the fish feed on in different situations and help him devise strategies for taking such fish. The pages of the practical-minded angler's *The Compleat Angler* will be well worn near the end of the book in Cotton's section; the less practical-minded angler's copy will have more bookmarks and notes scrawled in the margins of Walton's section. The well-read angler will have many other writers to select among in addition to Walton, and I'll leave it to those more widely read than me to publish a list of Best Angling Books someday. Probably such a list already exists and I simply haven't seen it yet.

For the sake of our fireside angler who may be getting drowsy in front of the warm fire—his stocking feet propped up on the hassock, his attention diverted by the snowflakes falling silently outside the window, soft white crystals thickening the dark December air—for his sake, let's consider only two other angling writers now: Norman Maclean and Roderick Haig-Brown. Both of these writers, who write about fishing in addition to other human affairs, create a mood that instantly envelopes you. If you want to be transported from your fireside reading chair, dig into these two and you will be on a Montana trout stream flanked by ponderosa pines or hip-deep in a British Columbia steelhead river hemmed in by tall red-barked cedars. You will be immersed not only in the pursuit of fish, but in the struggle to live a full and contented life as first prescribed by Walton. Maclean's narrator in *A River Runs Through It* struggles unsuccessfully to steer his errant brother's life on a less destructive course. Haig-Brown's books chronicle a life full of adventure, a life that is close to the natural world and close also to the lives of men and women and children who live in that world.

One curious aspect of the best angling literature is the creation of so many fine father images. Cotton may have started this with his references to his mentor Father Walton, thirty-seven years his senior. And Walton, age sixty when the first edition of *The Compleat Angler* was published, does seem a wonderful father figure, dispensing advice that is at once light-hearted and trenchant as he rattles off quotes from King Solomon to Montaigne. Maclean's old man narrator looks back on his early years with his father, a Presbyterian minister, and his younger brother Paul with a sadness, wisdom and a lyrical eloquence that is overwhelming by the final page. And who wouldn't strive to be the compassionate, virile, even-headed and yet spirited father that emerges from Haig-Brown's autobiographical writings about his life as an angling innovator, father, husband, writer, logger, frontier magistrate, naturalist and early conservationist.

But the fireside angler cannot read books and magazines forever. Eventually he strays over into the pile of mail-order catalogs that arrive largely unsolicited in the mail slot month after month. You get to a point in your angling life that you really don't need any more gear, but you still like to thumb through the catalogs. At times you surprise yourself at the quickening desire for more gear—unneeded but wanted. Already, you could outfit a good-sized fishing party with your spare gear alone and yet you notice an advertisement for a seven-foot, two-weight rod weighing little more than an ounce and a matching bantam-weight reel. You realize it would be just the ticket for those tiny lost creeks in the mountains, shrouded by dense riparian overhang and populated by brilliantly colored natives. Oh...you already have a four-weight trout rod. But it's seven *and a half feet* long and the reel is *awfully* heavy, and to really appreciate the beauty of those small trout streams you should lighten up.

Maps too are on the table, both for re-tracing past trips and planning new ones. If you like to do some of your fishing on backpacks you will spend considerable time with all manner of maps acquainting yourself with the country to be explored. Those who don't appreciate maps are forever amazed at how much time you can spend studying them. They don't realize that a good topographic map is much more than a road map. A topo map of the backcountry reveals the lay of the land and waters in three-dimensions in your imagination. You assess trail miles between destinations, loop routes, water sources, elevation, treeline, size of streams, gradient, and the shapes and depths of lakes. You're lost, gone, in another world and it is no longer winter in front of the fire: it's summer in the high country and the sparkling dark blue jewel of an alpine lake has just come into view. It is a calm day under a cerulean blue windless sky and the lake's mirror surface ripples with rise rings and you can't wait to get your pack rod assembled and out onto the water.

The fire ebbs, curling smoke out the chimney into the snowy sky overhead, not unlike the smoke that rises into the twinkling star sky from your high lakes campfire. The flames flicker yellow-orange and jagged-edged feeding on the wood that you placed on the andirons—prunings from the backyard cherry tree, an elm half from the neighbor's windfall last February and dead lilac branches from behind the garage. A fire in the hearth is an important part of the fireside angler, though you can rummage through your magazines, catalogs, books and maps without one. A fire in the hearth is like a fire at fishing camp, a beacon for reflection, a lure pulling you into the elemental. We anglers are an elemental lot, accustomed as we are to a world of water and air and earth: wading the big waters we stand felt-shoed on the wet rocky earth, feel the rush of water around our legs and double haul through air thick with fluttering caddis. Fire is a part of this too, both at home in our down time and on fishing trips.

The ability to make fire is one of the characteristics that separate us from animals. It provides us with physical and psychic comforts that we take for granted nowadays. But on a fishing trip, in cold weather, a fire's value is easy to appreciate. On winter steelhead floats, a lunchtime streamside fire is an important part of the day. Stow some newspaper and kindling in the dryhold of the driftboat and then gather driftwood when you're ready. If you're organized, you might have a pot along to heat water for soup or tea. The fire will warm those cold steelhead-er's fingers. And you can slip off your waders and warm your feet before the alder wood flames that hiss with the fall of mid-day snow. It seems a delightful luxury to get close to something hot on a cold fishing day. The lunch fire doesn't have to take a long time, but it will lift your spirits and invigorate your after-noon angling.

The fire in the fireplace has consumed its fuel, the alder and elm now fine gray ash and glowing coals. Overhead in the snow sky the clouds' moisture, the genesis of your rivers, condenses in the night-cooled air, the precipitation coming down as snow, the flakes quietly layering themselves one upon another on the asphalt street, the concrete sidewalk and the grass lawn. The lone ice cube in your glass has long since melted. You yawn and look at all the magazines and books and maps that you haven't yet touched tonight. But it's late and winter is long and there will be time for more fireside angling tomorrow.